EXECUTIVE
FREEDOM

EXECUTIVE FREEDOM

How to Escape the C-Suite, Create Income Security, and Take Back Control by Building a Part-Time Portfolio Career

Colin Mills & Sara Daw

BRIGHTFLAME BOOKS, TORONTO

Table of Contents

Preface

If you've ever wondered what part-time portfolio working is all about, this book is for you.

If you think portfolio working might be for you then, again, you've picked up the right book.

If you are currently a frustrated C-suite executive, fed up with being "owned" as an employee in the corporate world and wondering if that is all there is to your working life, again, you've arrived at the right place.

If you have already left a C-suite career and you are looking to build a portfolio lifestyle but feel stuck, it's worth reading on.

If you have retired—or are about to retire—from the C-suite, but you have the energy and the desire to do more, we show you how.

Finally, if you've worked in the C-suite, you took a career break, and now you are considering your alternatives, this book presents a real alternative for you to consider.

Colin Mills is the founder and current chairman of The Liberti Group, and The CFO Centre group of companies, including The FD Centre in the UK. Sara Daw is the CEO of those businesses. Together, we have built the world's largest providers of part-time portfolio C-suite executives from the ground up, incorporating around 1,000 top-talent finance, accounting, marketing, sales, HR, IT, and legal executives.

Based on our real-life experiences over eighteen years, and all the mistakes we learned from along the way, we share our stories with you of what this new world of working is all about.

Building on that experience and backed up with detailed research, we describe the different kinds of executive this new way of working most appeals to, the personal characteristics that help individuals succeed in this environment, and what it takes to make it in this new world, where you must surrender job security for income security.

In a nutshell, if you have C-suite experience, you should read this book. It might just change your life!

Colin Mills & Sara Daw

Necessity Is the Mother of Invention

Colin's Story

Sometimes, it's only when you really need to do something that you figure out a way to do it. In reality, of course, the answer or choice was there all along. It's just that sometimes you need a nudge to make you go looking.

And so, there I was in 2001.

After working my way up the corporate ladder from management trainee to the C-suite, I was the Group Chief Financial Officer (CFO) of a privately owned UK business and getting increasingly fed up with a way of life that was harming both my family and me.

I was in my early forties, making good money, but travelling too much, spending too much time away from home, and missing too many family events that meant something to my wife, Julie, and my children.

I had convinced myself that this was the only way to support our lifestyle, pay the mortgage, and buy the very best football boots for our four young boys, who were growing up fast.

I was wrong.

The grindstone of corporate life was wearing me down.

It was making me miserable.

And while my work ethic was strong, my performance was suffering with every day that passed.

As for home... God knows how I managed to stay married.

I felt controlled by my situation and my work position.

I had sold my soul to the corporation, and I knew it.

It was a form of "corporate slavery" that many senior executives, I later discovered, can relate to only too well.

This hadn't happened overnight, of course. It had crept up on me slowly, over several years. And while Julie and I had been discussing for a long time what we should be doing with the rest of our lives, the only concrete action we had taken was to start a small property development business on the side with some good friends. We hoped the venture would be profitable enough to gradually pay down our mortgage and relieve the pressure to stay in my corporate prison to earn a living.

I found great joy in starting that little business with Julie and our friends, and it encouraged me to think about what else I might do to achieve freedom away from corporate life.

Just as our first property development project was heading towards a successful conclusion, however, something else happened that abruptly caused me to take stock and changed my thinking forever.

My father died, suddenly and unexpectedly.

Necessity had come calling.

And it drove me to make dramatic changes to my work and lifestyle; to shift from corporate slavery to a more balanced, freedom-based lifestyle that would also provide interest, variety, challenge, enjoyment, and an acceptable income stream.

A hastily negotiated exit package and the profits from our first property venture gave us enough "financial runway" for me to test an idea I had been developing over the previous couple of years: becoming a part-time CFO and growing it into a business of part-time CFOs who were also seeking freedom for themselves.

I called that business The FD Centre[1], selling finance director/CFO services to mid-sized companies in the UK that didn't want, didn't need, and usually couldn't afford a full-time CFO, but required that skill set either on an ongoing basis or to address a specific situation that had arisen.

Sara's Story

I joined a Big Four audit practice in Bristol, UK after university. Upon qualifying as a chartered accountant, I moved into corporate finance and transaction advisory services in their London office. That's when I began to realise corporate life wasn't for me.

I resented being a slave to the corporate agenda and not in control of my destiny. The corporate dialogue and how we interacted among colleagues didn't feel "real". Everything seemed to be about who could work the longest hours to get a promotion. Besides, I was fed up working endless nights on transactions.

So, I joined a subsidiary of a large global corporation hoping that a switch from the accounting profession to working in industry would solve all my issues. For the first time in my career, I was finally able to look up from a spreadsheet and see all the other disciplines and functions

---

[1] In the UK, a CFO is more commonly referred to by the title financial director (FD), especially in SMEs

needed to run a business. I still had that feeling, however, of not really being free and having to wear a corporate mask every day. So, being someone who loves learning, I left to take my MBA at London Business School. I wanted to become more knowledgeable about business in general before deciding what to do next.

While my MBA gave me the business foundation I was looking for, it also made me even more attractive to the corporate world. Fortunately, my gut instinct told me that wasn't the right direction for me, and I started a consulting business with one of my professors and a few others. We built a small business with a core of global blue-chip clients, and I finally found—running an SME—that elusive "real" feeling I had been looking for, though it wasn't mirrored in our corporate clients.

At the start of my MBA, I had just got married, and now, four years later, Andrew and I had our first child, Gracie. Suddenly, I was a working mum, with a whole new set of challenges. I carried on working part-time and even had my first taste of being self-employed as an independent consultant. We hired a nanny to help with our childcare and by the time I became pregnant with our second daughter, Esme, I decided to take a career break: what's manageable with one child grew much trickier with two!

I decided to return to work when Esme was coming up to one, but not full-time. I didn't want to be travelling or commuting, and my experience building an SME had taught me that working with smaller and medium-sized businesses was far more attractive than a corporate employer in London.

The concept of 'part-time finance director' was just emerging at the time, so I decided to set myself up as one. My plan was to build a small portfolio of local clients so I could mix being a mum with fulfilling work. I was also excited by the thought that working this way, I was only as good as my last day's work and I must prove my worth as I go. The individuals and businesses I helped would truly value what I was doing for them!

While I felt certain I could find clients, I was nervous about whether I would be able to come up with all the answers and whether I would really feel connected to my clients and be part of their team.

I wanted a team—to feel supported and be part of something bigger—and Andrew suggested I look for others doing the same kind of work. It was early 2005 when I found The FD Centre, which Colin had set up a few years earlier, and the rest, as they say, is history. I joined The FD Centre with Colin and became busy building my portfolio of clients.

I could not have done this without Andrew. He supported our growing family financially as Colin and I built the UK business, and he believed in me every step of the way. That was a huge benefit, because once I had three stable clients—five or six days' work a month—I was able to spend the rest of my time on growing the company.

Balancing business growth and earning fees is a major dilemma for new executives: when you're on your own, you can't be 100% fee-earning and build a business at the same time. You have to set aside time for business development, which takes you away from servicing clients and making money. That's where being in a team-based organisation like a Liberti Group company is a significant advantage because there will be people like me who don't have the same pressure to be billable and can go out and build the business.

So that's how I started my portfolio. We even managed to fit in having our third daughter, Mabel. Better yet, my clients, some of whom were family businesses, totally understood what it is like to own and run a business while also being mum or dad.

I had finally found that "real" environment and sense of freedom I had been looking for.

And Today

As we write, that original business has expanded into 16 countries across 5 continents under the brand The CFO Centre Group, and there are now more than 600 CFOs who are benefitting from the Freedom Lifestyle first conceived some 18 years ago.

Additionally, with the creation of The Liberti Group (*liberti*: a Latin word meaning slaves who have been freed), we now offer part-time C-suite professionals to mid-sized businesses through:

- The CFO Centre/The FD Centre (finance directors)
- The Marketing Centre (marketing directors)
- Freeman Clarke (IT directors)
- People Puzzles (HR directors)
- Your Right Hand (financial controllers and bookkeepers)
- Kiss the Fish (sales directors, sales coaches, and sales trainers)
- My InHouse Lawyer (legal experts).

These niche C-suite businesses provide top-level talent to growing companies with ambitious owners who are seeking to scale up and cope with the problems that inevitably come up along the way.

That's over 1,000 professionals working across seven disciplines, all working for a portfolio of multiple clients in a team environment, creating freedom for themselves and—through the services they deliver—for their clients.

In many ways, our journey is just beginning. However, the stories of the hundreds of professionals who have joined us over the last 18 years have inspired us to share our progress so far and to show that Charles Handy was definitely onto something when he said, in his 1991 book *The Age of Unreason*, that the future of work would be characterized by shamrock organisations and portfolio workers.

Chapter One

The Idea

Much has been written in recent times about the future of work, portfolio lifestyles, and the gig economy as it relates to professionals. However, there has been very little real-world evidence of how to turn the theory into practice: what portfolio lifestyles look like, why they are attractive to professionals, what a business model built around portfolio lifestyles looks like, what the issues are, and what type of people it works for.

This book attempts in a small way to fill that gap.

Rather than just rely on our story, our biases, and our memories over 18 years, we set about making this as current and as real as possible by undertaking 12 months of dedicated research.

The Research

We broke our research down into three key stages.

1. We created a survey questionnaire to identify the following:
    a. What initially attracts professionals to this business model?
    b. What types of people are attracted to the business model?
    c. What issues are they most concerned about?
    d. What keeps them engaged with the business model once they are in?
2. We surveyed over 300 Liberti professionals who are currently operating the portfolio professional business model.
3. We selected 30 respondents and carried out in-depth interviews to get more in-depth views on the Liberti business model and what it takes to really succeed in building a portfolio.

The Analysis

As you can imagine, gathering the data from 300 busy professionals took time.

It was nothing, however, compared to the time it took to then analyse their responses and distil that data down into something simple to understand and present, but more importantly, something that we could use to inform our recruitment, induction, training, and our entire business model going forward.

The Magic Triangle

As we explored the data and combined it with the knowledge we had gained in developing a portfolio professional business model over the course of 18 years, simplicity gradually emerged from the complexity, and we saw a "magic triangle" develop that started to explain the future of work in terms of a team-based approach to portfolio working.

We identified:

1. Eight categories ("Key Personas") of people that are most attracted to team-based portfolio lifestyles

2. Six "Virtues" that these personas exemplify

3. Six "Attraction Magnets" that draw portfolio workers to this way of working, and two key "Turnoffs" that they

are most concerned about when considering or working in this new way.

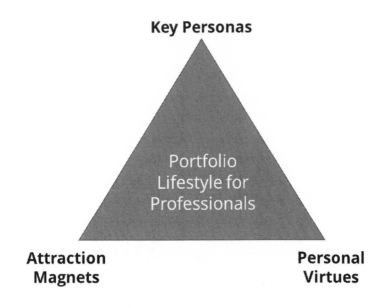

Team-Based Portfolio Working: The Magic Triangle

The 8 "Key Personas"

We found that people who are most attracted to portfolio professional working fall broadly into eight categories, which we call *key personas*.

In this section, we'll give a brief description of each persona. To bring the personas to life, however, we identified eights professionals inside Liberti Group who typify those personas and created in-depth case studies that illustrate what it takes to succeed in each type. You'll find the case studies in Chapter 3.

The Freedom Seeker

On the face of it, you are at the top of your career—you have the big title, the global board position, the international travel—and then one day you wake up and think "Why?" and you decide it's time to reclaim your life and live it on your own terms.

We have many Freedom Seekers in the business. Indeed, Colin himself was a Freedom Seeker, and it was one of his prime drivers for starting the business.

The Post-Kids Career Woman

You have a great career, and you've either reached the top, or you're well on your way. Then, child number one arrives, and you cope. Sort of. By the time child number two comes along, it all gets to be a bit too much. So, you decide to do things differently and look for an alternative.

Again, we have many Post-Kids Career Women in Liberti Group, including our CEO, Sara Daw.

The Mini Entrepreneur

You have a passion that you want to turn into a business, but you also have commitments that require something with more financial stability. A full-time job would keep you from pursuing your passion, but a portfolio career provides the perfect balance.

Liberti executives include a food blogger, a golf glove producer, a principal who runs an award-winning garden centre in Battersea, and many others.

The Work/Care Balancer

You have someone else who depends on you for care and support. A full-time position—especially one that matches your level of seniority—would place too many demands on your time and keep you away from home too much, so you need something with time flexibility that you can do locally.

We have a number of people in the business who joined because they are caring for someone in the family and can't commit to a full-on, full-time job.

The Independent Who Wants to be Part of Something

You've already been successful as an independent portfolio executive, but you value teamwork and being part of something bigger, and you're fed up with the peaks and troughs of working on your own.

One of our first CFOs in London, Bertie Maxwell, joined us after building a successful portfolio business on his own.

The Career Portfolioer

In your mid-30's to mid-40's, you see a portfolio lifestyle as a viable career alternative. While you need money, you value freedom, control and flexibility.

We increasingly see younger executives joining us as a credible and more attractive alternative to rising up through the hierarchy in a faceless corporation.

The Scale Up Enthusiast

You love the variety and interest of working with scale-ups—businesses that are beyond startup but are not yet a mature organization—and you get immense satisfaction from helping them grow to the next level

The Seasoned Veteran

You've been there, seen it, and done it. In your mid-50s to mid-60s, you're a veteran with a vast array of commercial experience over many years and many different economic cycles. You're not ready to retire, but employers just see a pension commitment they don't want to take on.

Corporations often don't see a place for these experienced executives. Yet we are all living longer and are healthier than ever before. These seasoned veterans have a lot to give to ambitious businesses, and they have the experience to show those businesses the way.

The 6 "Virtues"

Our research identified a mindset that the most successful portfolio workers exemplify. This way of working isn't for everyone, but it can achieve some remarkable success for individuals if they have the right mindset, which we distilled down to six Virtues or behaviours. Some people have these virtues naturally, but they can also be developed through effort and experience.

In Chapter 4 we explain and illustrate the mindset in depth, with specific examples. If you're considering this way of working, take a serious look at these traits and ask yourself how well you match up to them. For now, here's a very brief summary of each Virtue.

Humble

In his book *Ideal Team Player*, Patrick Lencioni identifies humility as the single greatest attribute of a "team player". Given that portfolio working involves working with multiple teams most of the time, it's perhaps no surprise that humility is equally critical for a portfolio executive.

When you walk into an SME to deliver part-time professional services, you have to leave your ego at the door. The kind of clients that need a portfolio executive usually don't much care what you've done before, which great companies you've worked for, or how technically competent you are. What they do care about is what you can do for them and whether you can fit into their world, their business, and their team.

Givers

In his book *Give and Take*, Adam Grant shows that people who give without expecting a favour in return are more successful in the long term.

Networked

Coming to the portfolio world with an extensive network is an enormous help and accelerator. If you don't have one, you can build one quickly as long as you realize how important it is to be networked.

People who genuinely believe in building authentic professional networks tend to be more successful in the long term. Networking isn't a numbers game; there has to be substance to the relationships you build.

Relationship

"It's all about the relationship."

Whether it's finding clients, winning clients, keeping clients, or working with your colleagues, everything you do in the portfolio world requires a relationship mindset.

Man, as they say, is not an island.

Learners

Personal success in the future of work is all about continuous learning, be that the acquisition of new hard or soft skills or learning from the unfamiliar situations you experience. Anyone who thinks they are too old to learn is probably not a good fit for this new world of work.

Hungry/Active

While this way of working will give you great freedom and flexibility, building and keeping a Portfolio is not for the faint-hearted.

One thing that stood out clearly in our research is that our most successful executives were all very active. You can't afford to sit in your armchair waiting for the phone to ring. You need to be hungry, constantly on the lookout for more things to do, more things to learn, and more responsibility to take on.

People who act like that also have an energy that clients love to connect with.

Six Attraction Magnets and Two Turn-Offs

In creating the survey, we started with a hypothesis about what attracted people to our business model and why. In the main, our views turned out to be correct. What did vary, however, was the relative emphasis that different professionals gave those factors.

We also identified areas that cause most concern to new Freedom-based workers, and—following a methodology set out in Mauborgne and Kim's book *Blue Ocean Strategy*—we created a strategy canvas comparing the Liberti business model to the most common alternatives: permanent employment, freelancing, and joining a business advisory franchise.

The insights we gained from this part of the study explain why the business model we created for portfolio working, based as it is on our own mistakes and real-life experience, has held up over time, and illustrate what matters most to professionals about the future of their own work.

The Six Attraction Magnets

1. Freedom

Hardly surprisingly, perhaps, the most important thing that attracted portfolio professionals to Liberti—and which keeps them with us—is the freedom it gives them to exercise control over their career and lifestyle choices.

The pursuit of freedom is why Colin set up the business in the first place, and it is still our purpose today. We designed the Liberti business model very carefully to give us that freedom from corporate life and to achieve more flexibility, variety, and control over how we spend our time.

In addition, we observed something that our clients are looking for also: Many entrepreneurs start their business to achieve more freedom and control over their lives. We align with that very closely and understand the purpose behind their decision to start a business.

So, as well as making our technical skills available to business owners, we also share their mindset around freedom and choice to spend our time doing more of the things we love and enabling us to be in that state author Mihaly Csikszentmihalyi calls "flow". When you are in flow, your skills and what you are doing is so aligned with who you are that it barely seems like work anymore.

2. Working with a Variety of SME Clients

Having access to a variety of SME clients was important to people, both initially and today. We are aiming to make a real difference to our clients, and our model enables us to work with a good range of SME businesses on a part-time basis throughout their lifecycle.

It means that no two days are ever the same: we have real variety throughout the week in the work we do, the technical issues and challenges we face, and the sector complexities, personalities, and cultures we have to deal with. One day we might be working at a client site where we have our own office, and another day we might be perched on the corner of a desk as that is the only available space. It is these situations which bring real colour to what we do each day, and over time we experience how we can improve these businesses and make a real difference.

People also saw working with a portfolio of clients as a way to de-risk their careers by making them less dependent on any one client, as well as developing their skill sets through new experiences and knowledge. Our respondents summed it up in comments like "it really challenges my intellect," and "I am helping a diverse group of businesses while being my own boss yet still very much part of a team."

3. Flexible Working and Work-Life Balance

Being able to work flexibly, with control over work-life balance was another important recurring theme that emerged from our survey.

We all have priorities in our life that we want to balance around our work, and we designed the Liberti model explicitly with this in mind. We wanted professionals to be able to bring their 'whole selves' to work, as we feel it enables us to deliver better in the long run for our clients (and of course, is much more enjoyable). So, we needed to find a model that accommodated and acknowledged that diversity in priorities.

This is illustrated well in the following survey response: *"In over 5 years, I have very rarely missed a school run, assembly, sports day, or special event, but my clients always see me on the days they request. If a meeting has to be early morning then I am still able to make it, which delivers the right level of service for my client, without it needing to be every single working day."*

SME clients also tend to be more accepting and understanding of the need for work-life balance than corporations, so again we are aligning ourselves with our client base.

Sara experienced this herself shortly after joining The FD Centre. She was pregnant with her third daughter, Mabel, and it was getting close to when she would need to take maternity leave. Sara wasn't planning to take much time off; instead, she intended to work part-time for a while. She discussed with a client how she was going to handle this period and the answer was, "Don't worry, I'll come over to your house when I need you. I've got two girls myself, so we can look after your little one while we have any discussions that we need to!"

And that is precisely what happened. It worked for both parties, and they were able to continue working together during that time.

Now, this arrangement isn't something that would work for every client, but it illustrates very well the point about flexible working and bringing our whole selves to work. We believe that to have fully engaged people at work, we need to fully engage with each individual and with what works for us both in and out of work.

4. Open and Fair Business Model

Liberti is fully transparent about the commercial business model and how it works. We share openly how client fees are split between everyone involved in delivering value to the client, and we have worked hard to ensure it is a fair allocation that rewards all the parties appropriately for their contribution to making the business work.

What was interesting was that portfolio workers really appreciated this openness and honesty both when they were joining and once they were in the business.

We feel that, energetically, it is essential for us all to share fees in an agreed way as we earn them. The approach means that everyone contributes to finding, winning and keeping clients with team support, so everyone advances across the whole business model and learns the skills they need to build a portfolio of clients to the level they want and keep it there.

This comes from our belief that if we all learn these skills and work together, we will de-risk our careers.

5. Sales and Marketing System that delivers results

Respondents saw the sales and marketing system as a benefit of joining and staying in The Liberti Group. Everyone we asked realized that, while it was essential to have the best product in the marketplace, if you can't access the market then the quality of the product is irrelevant.

Over the years, our business has focused on building many channels to market so that we are not dependent on any one channel. People clearly recognized that central channels—activities that each Liberti company undertakes on behalf of everyone in the business, such as digital marketing, social media, email marketing, advertising, direct mail, and PR—are as critical to ensuring the flow of work to our executives as the marketing channels we train them to implement for themselves, such as "street marketing" (our take on advanced networking), distribution (a team-centred approach to developing relationships with other professional firms), events, and client referrals.

We are always innovating in response to changing market conditions—testing new channels and optimising existing ones—and this was a huge attractor to portfolio professionals seeking to build a career and an income stream in this industry.

Across Liberti, we generate over 1,000 opportunities every quarter, so our marketing system is provably delivering. The challenge is to balance central and regional activities and to maintain momentum across all the channels, as that is what drives the results.

In addition, the marketing we do is not just about finding and winning—keeping is a critical part of our sales and marketing system.

6. Team

Most professionals love being part of a team, and this came across strongly in our research. While standing out and being successful (whatever success means to each individual) is essential, being part of something bigger, having colleagues around you (even if the connection is virtual), and being able to tap into a collegiate support network of like-minded individuals who are all part of the same team also matter to professionals. Of course, some professionals are happy to work alone, but for the most part, there is a sense of security that comes from being part of a pack, tribe, or team.

The Two Turn-Offs

Inevitably, there are some downsides when it comes to building a portfolio, and two aspects, in particular, were of most concern to professionals.

1. Uncertainty of Income Stream

The feeling of insecurity and uncertainty of income came across as a critical concern for our portfolio professionals. This was especially true in the start-up period, when you're building a book of clients.

Despite the upsides, portfolio working, even for professionals with high skill levels, has its drawbacks. Having a financial runway—that is, having sufficient funds to survive a period of zero or low income—is a requisite for this lifestyle. Of course, how long that period will be depends in great measure on you and on the portfolio organization you join—be it The Liberti Group or someone else.

It was clear that, even when workers are able to build a portfolio of clients quickly, the uncertainty takes some getting used to, even though a portfolio of clients de-risks your income to an extent and can provide much more certainly over time than traditional employment models.

2. Getting used to this way of Working

For a highly experienced professional coming out of a corporate environment, the challenges of starting a new enterprise—taking care of your own billing and compliance requirements with less admin support than you may be used to, and even the realisation of what it really means to be more self-sufficient and manage your time across a number of clients—can be daunting.

And it can easily overwhelm you when you couple all that with the need to participate actively in the marketing process, sell yourself during sales meetings, and spend time building relationships with mid-tier business owners (who can sometimes be challenging).

It was clear from our survey that, despite all the conversations we have up front with prospective executives about the realities of the lifestyle and the constant learning required (especially in non-technical topics), it's often only when you face the harsh reality of making your own coffee that you understand the implications of what you have let yourself in for.

As we said earlier, the team-based portfolio professional lifestyle isn't for everyone. It wasn't designed to be. It does, however, work extremely well for those who love freedom, variety, flexibility, challenge, and a team environment, and who can adapt to the realities of what it takes to achieve those benefits.

The rest of this book details the magic triangle model of team-based portfolio lifestyles for professionals, with stories, illustrations, and anecdotes that will hopefully bring the future of work to life for all those that might be interested.

Chapter 2

The Portfolio Gig Economy for Professionals is Here

This chapter briefly sets the scene and highlights the drivers towards team-based portfolio working and the future of work. We show that, in some respects, that future is already here, and draw comparisons between different ways of working for professionals. Finally, we offer a leadership approach for this new world.

If you've read any of the many recent books on the future of work, you could be forgiven for being confused about what is driving that future. Rather than list the dozens of trends and shifts affecting employment and work, we have identified the four that are most relevant to the future of work as it relates to the portfolio world:

1. Demographics
2. Belonging
3. Technology
4. Globalisation

1. Demographics

Two important demographic shifts directly impact the future of work and the rise in portfolio working.

The first is a growing tendency for older workers to delay retirement either completely (by staying in their job or taking a new one) or partially (by working part-time). An article in The Times (August 2017) suggests that "Older-preneurs insist retirement is for wimps" and contends that Britons appear to have little appetite for taking things easy as they grow older. At the same time, a study by Barclays Bank reports that the number of businesses run by people over the age of 55 has increased by more than 63% over the past decade.

This trend for older people to become their own boss may be driven by the inadequacy of many pensions, or it may simply be that older generations are healthier than previous generations and often wish to put their skills and experience to profitable use but want to work flexible hours.

Whatever is behind it, it seems clear that this trend will continue. Lynda Gratton, in her book *The Shift* (2011), predicts that the coming decades will be defined by the largest demographic group the world has ever seen, the baby boomers (those born between 1946 and 1964). That period saw around 77 million babies born in the USA, while birth rates in many European countries reached as high as 20 per thousand—nearly five times the 2010 rate.

By 2025, most of those baby boomers will have left the "traditional" workforce, taking with them a huge store of knowledge and know-how. That will probably create severe skill shortages, and companies will be looking for ways to hold onto that knowledge.

Combine this with the fact that "Olderpreneurs" are living longer, are healthier, and need to top up their pensions, and you arrive at the conclusion that more flexible forms of working will continue to develop.

We have observed this trend directly within The Liberti Group. In our 2017 survey, we found that 15% of the professionals in Liberti describe themselves as "seasoned professionals" past normal retirement age and with a vast array of experience gained over many different economic cycles.

At the other end of the age spectrum, the second big change in the workforce is the growing proportion of the workforce accounted for by people born between 1980 and 2000, popularly referred to as "Gen Y" or "millennials". Members of that generation have views, needs, and expectations of work that are very different from those of their Gen X and baby boomer bosses, and those older generations are struggling to adapt.

Generations by Year of Birth

Demographic	Born
Baby Boomers	1946 – 1964
Generation X	1964 – 1980
Generation Y/Millennials	1980 – 2000
Generation Z	After 2000

According to the UK Office of National Statistics, there are around 18 million millennials in the UK. Even allowing for the fact that some of them may be unemployed, that's a significant proportion of the UK's active workforce of 31 million people.

A December 2016 report by UK Vistage (a peer-to-peer CEO networking organization) attempted to summarise the characteristics of the millennial generation. Given that every new recruit to a company under the age of 39 falls into this category, understanding how they think and what they demand from their working life is becoming critical in shaping the future of work.

While the Vistage report acknowledged the dangers of attempting to summarise the attitudes of an entire generation, they did identify some broad features that characterise millennials.

Millennials value empowerment to get things done. They want challenging work, collaboration, teamwork, and fun. They seek responsibility for their own personal development. The boundary between work and life becomes more blurred for millennials, and while they accept that the need for money is an inevitable fact of life, they are rather less motivated by it than previous generations. More importantly, they are not prepared to sacrifice everything else in pursuit of wealth.

Gustavo Grodnitzky, the author of *Culture Trumps Everything*, sums it up perfectly: for Gen Y "money is a threshold, not a scorecard."

Since money is not the be-all and end-all, millennials care more about work-life balance than their parents, who they've watched as they've grown up doing stressful corporate jobs. They care more about experiences than materialistic "stuff" or scrimping together a deposit to buy their own property.

Indeed, when it comes to work-life balance, the single most important element for millennials is that they want autonomy to work when and how they choose; they want control over their lives, and they value flexibility highly.

Millennials also care deeply about causes—"why" is a major motivator for them. They want to know why companies are doing the things they do, and how this contributes to society and the environment.

When it comes to jobs, they don't understand the concept of the career ladder. They are much more likely than earlier generations to "job hop", and many want to start their own business.

In demographic terms, then, there are two big waves at both extremes of the workforce that will determine the future of work: the baby boomers, who will be working past normal retirement, and the millennials, who have a different attitude towards how they work and live.

It turns out, however, that one thing unites these generations: the desire for flexibility.

Increasingly, fathers want to be more hands-on with their children and therefore seek flexible and part-time employment opportunities. Mothers, for their part, want to be able to re-enter the workforce at a level of commitment and intensity that suits them.

Having seen their boomer parents sacrifice everything for career advancement, Gen Y is increasingly focused on work-life balance, with flexibility at the top of their list of requirements.

Finally, those older workers who are retiring later want flexibility during those additional active years to work hours that suit them.

The responses we collected in the research for this book supported Vistage's report on the future of work strongly.

The overriding reason why professionals connect with the Liberti model is to achieve freedom and flexibility in their working patterns. Of course, there were other key drivers, but this was at the top of the list.

2. Belonging

"No man is an island," said John Donne, "entire of itself".

We need others in order to feel wanted and useful, loved if possible, and connected to the world.

Here is Charles Handy in his book *The Second Curve— Thoughts on Reinventing Society.*

> *And in the future the whole idea of taking control of one's life and having freedom and flexibility to do what you want, where you want, when you want creates a paradox, with man's natural want to be part of something. Loneliness doesn't sit well for most of us, and being part of a team is natural.*

It seems that loneliness of one sort or another is a big issue for many of us. Handy goes on to suggest that loneliness engenders a feeling of not mattering much to anyone, and of going unnoticed in the world. This has major implications for the future of work for professionals in that, while freelancing and independence themselves can give us flex-ibility and freedom, they can also create a form of loneli-ness that feels uncomfortable to many of us.

We observed this from the very earliest stages of building the Liberti business. When one of our first part-time fi-nance directors joined us, he had been working as an in-dependent freelancer and had built up a portfolio of cli-ents over several years. He was, by any measure, success-ful.

So, why did he join us?

Because he was lonely.

Yes, he had been dealing with the feast-and-famine that most freelancers face, but his main reason for connecting with The FD Centre (the original Liberti business) was that he wanted to be part of something bigger. He wanted to work with like-minded individuals, to chat about the issues we all had, to compare notes on different alternative strategies for our clients, and to be able to discuss what we were doing to deliver success for our clients and our-selves. He wanted, in other words, to operate in a colle-giate environment.

As Abraham Maslow described as far back as 1943, humans share a set of common overarching needs that drive everything we do. We seek safety for ourselves and those we love. We like to be cherished and find a sense of belonging in the communities we live in. We need a sense of achievement and of a job well done. And for some, we also want a sense of what he called self-actualization—the feeling that we have done our best and have fulfilled our potential.

Not everyone will want to be part of a team in their working life, but most will, because being part of a community and having that sense of belonging is human nature.

3. Technology

Technology has already changed the face of work everywhere from the factory floor to the front and back office. Automation will continue to displace an increasing number of jobs, including more and more "professional" roles.

The most significant impact technology is likely to have on professional workers, however, is in how they engage with their employers and clients, and by enabling increasing levels of flexibility, freeing employees from the shackles of the traditional workplace.

Advances in communication, social interaction, and methods of collaboration will drive the future of work as we move increasingly towards a virtual world.

In our own business, which operates in 16 countries spread across numerous time zones, we spend a significant part of our week talking to people around the world through Skype, Facetime, Zoom, and other remote communication applications in ways that wouldn't have been feasible just a few years ago, when remote communication was complicated, expensive, and unreliable. Today it can be done simply and with little or no cost.

Technology has also changed social interaction within the business. Our professionals connect with each other through instant messaging apps like WhatsApp almost as conveniently as if they were in the same room. And for millennials, these ways of communicating are the norm.

Finally, how we collaborate across the business regionally, nationally, and internationally has changed. By incorporating Google Drive, Dropbox, Sharepoint, and similar file-sharing platforms, we make it possible for our professionals to work together on documents wherever they are in the world.

Essentially, technology has made it easier than ever for team members to work together whatever their location.

4. Globalisation

Ask any business person to name one thing that has most changed the business environment in recent years and what is most likely to change business in the future, and their answer to both will probably be globalisation.

Globalisation has allowed The Liberti Group itself to expand rapidly outside of the UK. We now have teams servicing clients in 16 countries across 5 continents, with data research teams in India and admin teams in the Philippines.

The powerful combination of globalisation and technology has made the world a much smaller place—a trend that will undoubtedly continue into the future—and today, even the smallest business is able to do business around the world without boundaries.

The Future of Work for Professionals is already here

Given the interaction of the four factors I described above—demographics, belonging, technology and globalisation—it's no wonder that more flexible ways of working, more agile forms of organization structure, and new work environments have already arisen in the professional services marketplace and others.

For professionals, the future of work is already through a number of different models, albeit at relatively early stages of development.

And yet, even as far back as 1991, management writer Charles Handy set out his vision of the types of organization that would evolve in the future in his book *The Age Of Unreason.*

When Colin was designing the structure and setup of our firm in 2001, he read Handy's predictions with keen interest, and our own business model was partly structured on Handy's thinking, in particular the concept he called the "shamrock" organization.

The Shamrock Organisation

The shamrock—the national emblem of Ireland—is a visual metaphor for an organization with three "leafs". The first leaf consists of a small nucleus of highly paid full-time professionals, technicians, and managers. Handy called these "core workers".

The second leaf is all the non-essential speciality work which could be done by someone else, and therefore can be contracted out.

Finally, the third leaf is a flexible workforce of part-time and temporary workers who are there to cope with the peaks of demand that a company would experience from time to time. They are typically at the lower end of the skill range, with low costs and low benefits.

Today, you can see this model in many organisations, particularly professional services firms.

The Rise of the Supertemp

The Rise of the Supertemp is a landmark Harvard Business Review article from 2012 which argues that the best executive and professional jobs may no longer be full-time "gigs". It predicted, in other words, the gig economy for professionals and executives.

Jody Greenstone Miller and Matt Miller describe Supertemps as top managers and professionals, from lawyers to CFOs to consultants. They are refugees from big corporations and professional firms who value the autonomy and flexibility of temporary or project-based work and find the compensation comparable to what they earned in full-time jobs, sometimes even better.

The Millers go on to quote Dan Pink, who told them "it isn't a bunch of people who couldn't get a job anywhere. It used to be that someone who was out on their own was 'between jobs'. Now it's the people who have the power in the talent market who are going that way."

Consulting seems to be the area of professional services where these new forms of working are taking hold most rapidly. In another Harvard Business Review article from 2013, *Consulting on the Cusp of Disruption*, Clayton Christensen and his co-authors compare traditional consulting firms and what they do to examples of new firms who have developed more disruptive gig-based models which facilitate lower-cost services to clients yet still provide access to exceptional talent that is attracted by more flexible working.

These "facilitated networks" as Christensen describes them include OpenIDEO, CEB, Gerson Lehrman Group, Eden McCallum and BTG. These consulting firms, however, typically work with larger organizations; in our experience, very few firms are providing top-level talent to SMEs.

And this gig economy for white-collar workers is not a flash in the pan—it is a trend that will be with us well into the future. The Economist's January 2015 Future of Work briefing includes a feature, *Workers on Tap*, which describes in detail how freelance professional workers will reshape the nature of companies and the structure of their careers.

Additionally, *When The Gig Economy Meets Professional Services*, a 2017 seminar held at London Business School (LBS) confirms that the gig economy for professionals is here to stay. In the first session, Julian Birkinshaw, professor of strategy and entrepreneurship at LBS, shared research from the Royal Society of Arts indicating that 60% of the estimated 1.1 million workers in the gig economy in the UK are professionals—consultants, lawyers, executive coaches, designers, and IT specialists—enjoying a happy, flexible, freelance life.

Professional Services Business Models Compared

The case for implementing more flexible ways of working and organising firms as a way to attract top talent is compelling, and changes are already happening, primarily in professional firms and intermediaries that work with larger customers. There is strong demand for top talent from customers of all types. While intermediary firms like BTG, Eden McCallum, and others have focused on providing that top talent to large companies, however, the SME sector—as it often the case—has mostly been neglected. Yet in all developed nations, it is the SME sector that drives economic growth and development.

Below, we compare the team-based portfolio model to the three most common business models in the professional services industry: employment, franchising, and freelancing. To make the differences and similarities easier to see and understand, we create what Kim and Mauborgne, in their book *Blue Ocean Strategy*, call a strategy canvas.

If you're reading this book, we'll assume you are interested in working as a portfolio executive now or in the future. If so, you will be well armed in considering which might be the best way of working for you. If you are not interested in working in this space, you will still benefit from understanding how the different models work and what attracts talent to work in this industry.

Strategy Canvas: The Future of Work for Professionals

Comparing these different working alternatives for professionals highlights some interesting points. First, it's clear that there is a marked difference between full employment and hanging out a "single shingle" as an independent or freelancer. In particular, employment provides a degree of income stability that is missing from solo models of working.

This income stability is one of the major elements of what many people consider "job security"—something that employment is typically assumed to provide, and that working in your own business is presumed to lack. And yet, in the current working environment, we can legitimately question the whole concept of job security.

Diane Mulcahy, in her book *The Gig Economy*, boldly declares that there is no such thing as job security any more, and because of that, a job is no longer a viable foundation on which to build our professional, personal, or financial lives.

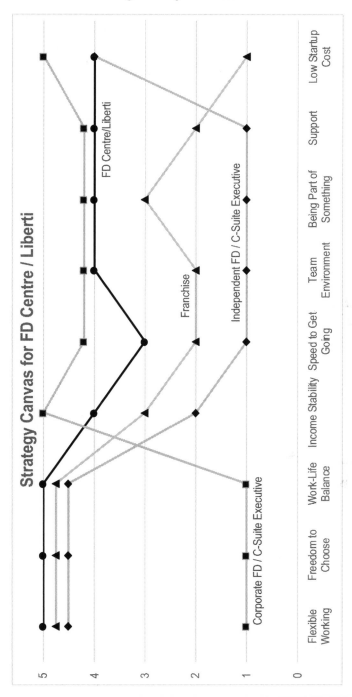

Strategy Canvas for FD Centre / Liberti

Nevertheless, there's something about a job—having someone else sign your paycheque—that makes most people feel more secure. The price they pay for that false sense of security, of course, is low freedom and flexibility: precisely the areas where independent working scores highly.

Against either of those, we have what we might call hybrid approaches: franchising and the team-based Liberti model.

Franchising offers the freedom many professionals crave and at the same time provides some of the support that you find in more traditional forms of employment. The key downside, however, is that franchisors require a financial payment up front, and most also demand monthly fees.

The other issue is how much support franchisors actually provide, both to get going and to support ongoing income streams.

With product franchises (the classic example being McDonald's), extensive support is provided that has been developed and perfected—often over many years—in the form of operations manuals to support the manufacture or servicing of the product, tried and tested advertising, marketing techniques, etc. However, product franchises do not typically require high skill levels.

In professional services, by contrast, performance depends much more on the individual's skill set and, as we have already shown, virtues and mindsets.

The team-based portfolio model developed by The Liberti Group shares with the franchise model a systematic way of doing things and central support particularly, in the case of Liberti, in terms of the sales and marketing aspects of developing a portfolio of clients and the strong teamwork that exists.

Sales and marketing is often a weakness in firms selling professional services. When Colin started the business, someone said to him, "Colin, you may be a talented CFO, and you may have done some brilliant things and worked for some marvellous companies in the past. But clients out there aren't interested in what you've done in the past. What they are interested in is what you can do for them now and in the future. And unless you can get in front of the client and convince them of that, you won't sell a thing."

A very significant difference between franchising and the Liberti model is that Liberti Group companies don't require an upfront capital investment. We select candidates based on a detailed assessment of the skill set and mindset needed to live a portfolio life rather than whether they have the money to pay a franchise fee.

The Liberti team-based portfolio professional model also provides similar freedom to life as an independent.

For most professionals, speed to get going and the certainty of income streams are without a doubt the biggest issues with the freelancing, franchising and Liberti models. Although, in the case of the latter, our assessment is that the Liberti model—with its dedicated sales and marketing experts, intensive training to support the startup phase, and ongoing training every year—provides improved certainty and speed to get going.

In the Liberti portfolio professional model particularly, once you're through the startup phase, you de-risk your income and create what Mulcahy calls *income* security rather than *job* security.

Income security is the strongest security we can create for ourselves. If we are confident we can generate the income we need to support the lifestyle we want, we feel more secure, regardless of our employment status.

In many ways, "employment" is just a state of mind.

Leadership in This New World

This evolution in the world of work clearly has an impact on the senior management of an organization and creates challenges for adapting to this new world. Old "command

and control" forms of management are much less relevant in a world characterised by flexible working, increasing numbers of experienced older professionals who have "been there, seen that, and got the T-shirt", and the growing impact of millennials, who simply don't buy into command and control structures.

Our view on leadership is heavily influenced by what we see works in our own firm, where these factors are already in play. We believe leadership by inspiration is the most effective form of leadership for this new environment, and it is the approach we have adopted.

The old leadership approach was highly autocratic, and authority was bestowed by an individual's place on the corporate ladder. In the new world, the leader's role is more like the conductor of the orchestra, bringing together the skills of the different generations within the business and coaching workers to draw the best out of them.

Above all, leaders in the new world must learn to "let go".

Chapter 3
The 8 Key Personas

In the rest of this book, we set out what drives top talent to join this industry, the types of people who are likely to excel, and the fundamentals of a business model that can match strong demand in the marketplace to top talent that want to work in a flexible manner yet benefit from a collegiate team-based approach.

As we discussed earlier in this book, in the course of our research, we found that people entering the portfolio industry tend to share some common characteristics and objectives. They are by no means universal, however, and executives broadly fell into eight categories, which we've labelled the *key personas*:

- Freedom Seeker
- Post-Kids Career Woman
- Mini Entrepreneur
- Work/Care Balancer
- Independent Who Wants to be Part of Something
- Career Portfolioer
- Scaleup Enthusiast

- Seasoned Veteran

We've also included a brief description of the main characteristics of each person before each interview.

The Freedom Seeker – Gill Banham

On the face of it, you are at the top of your career—you have the "big" title, the global board position, the international travel—and then one day you wake up and think "Why?" and you decide it's time to reclaim your life and live it on your own terms.

What were you doing before this?

I joined People Puzzles in March 2015. It was still relatively small at that point, and I was the first HR director recruited for our East of England region. I'd previously been the HR director for a multinational company that operated franchised luxury car dealerships.

I was with that company for twenty years and had seen four CEOs come and go in that time. Like all retail operations, it was an aggressive sales environment and, despite high turnover, net profits were low. HR often struggles in those kinds of organizations because it's not a revenue-generating channel and we're usually stereotyped as "soft".

What attracted you to a portfolio career?

My colleagues on the board of directors were typical type-A personalities, and so, even though I loved the company, in the end, I got tired of the constant boardroom battles to be heard and appreciated. I knew I wanted something different—I just didn't know what that "something" was.

Like many directors in large companies, I was working seven days a week, even when I was supposed to be on vacation. So, I wanted something part-time.

I saw an advert for People Puzzles that said they were looking for "part-time HR directors" and I responded, thinking that it would be two or three days a week. When the two founders, Ali and Helen, explained the portfolio lifestyle and what was involved, however, I immediately saw the possibilities.

What were the main drivers for joining a team rather than staying as an independent?

In corporate life, I had always been part of a team, and I enjoyed that, so I never wanted to be an independent consultant or contractor.

The way People Puzzles operated was fascinating to me. I could see there were risks—I was walking away from a successful career and doing something that was completely different—but I wanted more input and more control, and I wanted to work with nice people and to feel positive about my job.

That was a direct match to the ethos at People Puzzles: Ali and Helen are very clear that they want to work with "nice" companies, and that they want every HR director to be comfortable with their clients. If you're not comfortable, they'd rather you pull back and let another director step in who is a better cultural fit for the client. It's an approach that works well, and one of my clients is a company where one of my colleagues wasn't comfortable: a retail organisation with an aggressive sales environment!

I started off working five days a week, which meant I inevitably brought work home at weekends—old habits die hard—but now I've cut that back to a much more manageable three or four days a week, which is perfect.

What were the hardest aspects of transition?

Because of the way the induction process is managed at People Puzzles, the transition was actually easier than I thought it would be. In corporate life, there's a lot of structure, and I thought I would miss that, especially going from having a team of more than 20 people to being on my own. But there was a lot of contact throughout the induction period, and that made everything much smoother.

Financially, I had a lump sum of money in place, which also made things more comfortable as I didn't face the financial pressure that many new executives feel.

In the end, though, I didn't even need that as I found my first client within a couple of weeks. People Puzzles had been working on building the region, so they were already speaking to potential clients, and while I got started with the first one, Helen was lining up more clients for me.

My biggest concern was how to keep the momentum going. Our rates can seem high to smaller clients, so I was worried that as soon as I'd solved whatever problem they brought me in to address, I'd be out and looking for a new client. In fact, however, what happens is that as you work with each new client, you develop an ongoing relationship with the company.

At the same time, there are clients where part of my work has been to recruit someone more junior. They needed someone at my level initially. But going forwards they just needed an HR manager to keep things running. So there is a natural lifecycle to client engagement.

How long did it take you to get up and running and be confident that this was going to last?

I've had quiet periods, like any other new business, but because of the sales and marketing effort that People Puzzles and my regional director are constantly doing in the background, I've always had clients. That works well for me because, like most HR professionals, sales prospecting and cold calling aren't something I relish having to do. I'm paying for that marketing through the fee-sharing structure, so I take full advantage of it.

I know that if I can get in front of a prospect in a sales meeting, I can close them: it's that initial lead generation that I don't like. But because I could see all of that central prospecting activity, and I was confident that the People Puzzles team could find potential clients and get me in front of them. That in turn gave me confidence that the business was going to work.

How has it compared to your expectations?

I was quite cynical at the start. In many ways, it all sounded too good to be true. Here was an organization promising me that I could be independent and run my own business all while being part of a bigger entity that would provide help and support.

One particularly important aspect is the ability to get help from other HR professionals. We tend to be generalists in this industry, and it's not unusual to come across a situation you've never encountered. When that happens, I can email my colleagues and ask if anyone has dealt with something similar in the past, and people are only too happy to share not just their experience but their resources. For example, I might ask if anyone has delivered a leadership development workshop and somebody will send me their slide deck and workbooks.

It's incredibly comforting to know that there are other people out there who are in exactly the same boat. We all acknowledge that we can't know everything there is to know about HR, and we are happy to help each other.

What do you enjoy most about this lifestyle?

I most appreciate the balance. I'm a very independent person. I like working alone and not having to worry about having a team beneath me, but I also like knowing there's a safety net. Also, there are times when I'm busy, and no-one will mind if I retreat into myself and focus entirely on my clients. Then, when things are calmer, I can share and collaborate with my colleagues and help them out.

Another thing I love is being able to build very positive relationships with my clients. For example, one of the companies I work with has been with me almost from the start. I work one day a week for them, I am on their board, and I feel like part of the organization rather than a hired hand. I'm making a real difference to them, and it's lovely.

At home, my husband and I do more things together than we ever could when I was in the corporate world—even something as mundane as just taking a break to go out for lunch together.

What do you miss most about your old career?

I loved the company I worked for and my team, and I do miss them both. I also miss the prestige of working for a major corporation with a well-known brand. When people asked me what I did, it was easy to explain, and most people had heard of the company or one of our operating names. Not having that perceived status any more was a bit of a shock initially. Very few people I spoke to had heard of People Puzzles or even understood what a portfolio HR executive was.

What advice would you give someone else considering this lifestyle?

Plan ahead. Although my own transition was relatively painless, I know that many of my colleagues had a much harder time of it. Allow for at least 3-6 months where you're getting established and you're not going to be very busy with paid work. The end result is worth it, but you need resilience and determination to get there.

Alongside that, have a financial nest egg in place. Many people come into the profession but exit very quickly because the financial pressure is too great.

The Post-Kids Career Woman – Zara Merricks

You have a great career, and you've either reached the top or you're well on your way. Then, child number one arrives, and you cope. Sort of. By the time child number two comes along, it all gets to be a bit too much. So, you decide to do things differently and look for an alternative.

What were you doing before?

I was a finance director in an air freight business for five years. After I had my children, I took a couple of years off. What I found, though, was that I didn't cope well with being a full-time mum; I had the career bug. So, I started up on my own as a freelancer. The children were very young, so I was only working two days a week—enough to keep my brain active.

After eighteen months, I went back into industry full-time. When my marriage broke down a short time later, however, I went back to working part-time as a freelancer so that I could balance work, childcare, and my children.

I worked alone as a portfolio finance director for nine months before I found The FD Centre on LinkedIn. That was very lonely. Everything in my business was happening very locally, and I missed the community and support you get inside a company. There were days when I would get up, I'd work all day in my home office, and I wouldn't leave the house. I'm a social person, and I needed human interaction.

Through The FD Centre, I have clients far and wide, and I'm very busy servicing them (which is a good thing!). But there is a lot of internal networking, and I go to events—which you don't get to do when it's just you. I also enjoy networking with other businesses, so I'm always agreeing to go to external events. If anything, I'm getting too much social interaction these days!

What were the hardest aspects of making the transition from being on your own?

Like most new portfolio executives, I was frustrated by the time it took to get going. I'd assumed—and everybody does—that I was going to walk in and they would hand me a client on a plate. All through induction, everyone is telling you it will take a while for the business to build up, but you don't listen. You tell yourself you can buck the trend.

In the end, it was three months before I got a client over the line. It was a business I sourced for myself, just as I was getting to the point where I was thinking, *It's not happening for me.* Unlike a lot of professionals, though, I don't mind selling, so I was happy to go out and source my own clients.

I had a lot of frustrating experiences in the first three months—slow starters where I would have a couple of meetings, they'd sign up, and then they wouldn't start—and then everything came together at the same time.

Most of the executives I've spoken to had a similar experience: they have a long period with nothing, and then it's almost like someone flicks a switch and they get very busy.

What helped make the transition easier?

My regional director, Nick, was a big help. Once you've got your first client and the regional director knows who you are, what you like, and what clients suit you, it flows easily.

I'm a very open, honest person, and I speak my mind, so I have a good relationship with the regional director. It also helped that I had the experience of building my own business. One of the things people struggle with is juggling the demands of multiple clients. I understood how important diary management is when every client employs you on a part-time basis but wants to speak to you as though you were full-time: they all act as though they are your only client.

The induction process also helped. I was in a group of people just like me from across all the regions. Then for six weeks after induction, we had weekly "accelerator" sessions where you got to talk to the same people you were inducted with for about six weeks: everyone in the same situation, discussing what's going on for them, and helping each other.

How does it compare to your expectations?

It has exceeded my expectations. Going in, I was worried I was going to be the sole 40-something woman in a company full of men in their 60s and 70s and that I wouldn't have the level of experience needed. In fact, my background in the SME market was perfect, and I have a range of clients I love that I fitted into straight away.

What do you enjoy most about this lifestyle?

I love being able to choose when I do and don't work. I'm a single mum, and I need to make sure I can be available for the kids. So, having the flexibility to manage my own diary is very important, and I can block out days when I don't want to work.

Once you have a great relationship with your clients, they are usually very accommodating. For example, I always wanted to be able to take my children to school and wave them goodbye. All my clients are happy to let me take the kids to school and start after the school run. If I arrive half an hour late for the start of the day, they know I'm putting in the time somewhere else anyway. I'm probably giving more than I should, but in return, I'm working for some lovely people, so it works for us both.

What do you miss most about your old career?

I don't think there is anything I miss anymore. I am generally a lot happier in this lifestyle than I was before.

What I *don't* miss are the hassle and the office politics. As a director of a company with fifty staff, probably an hour of my day was spent listening to employees moaning at me about something or other. I don't get that any more. And I never get involved in the politics because I'm not there enough.

What advice would you give someone else considering this lifestyle?

Being a portfolio executive is more rewarding than being in one company day in and day out. It gets frustrating when you're a company director trying to make changes, but nothing's happening and you're fighting the same battles day in and day out. A major benefit of the portfolio lifestyle, in contrast, is that you really can make things happen.

To your clients, you are a cost, and they want to see a return on that cost. So, they do implement your advice, and often you can see the impact you're having almost immediately, which is very rewarding.

The Mini Entrepreneur – James Christian

You have a passion that you want to turn into a business, but you also have commitments that require something with more financial stability. A full-time job would keep you from pursuing your passion, but a portfolio career provides the perfect balance.

What were you doing before?

I joined The FD Centre two years ago after being COO of an agricultural company for five years and finance director of the same company for five years before that. One day my boss said to me, "I don't know if you want to be a great finance director or a CEO." I said, "I might as well be a CEO," and when he became the CEO himself he took me up with him and made me COO, which meant he got all the glory and I got all the pain!

My introduction to The FD Centre was a little circuitous. In 2016, I was planning to set up my own business to service agricultural companies.

As part of my preparation, I was looking around at various websites for inspiration, and I had found a site I really liked the look of and how they described what they did. I was talking to someone who had done some part-time work for us, and he suggested I look at The FD Centre— it turned out it was the site I'd found that I really liked.

So I thought, *Why bother reinventing the wheel? I may as well go straight to them.*

What attracted you to the portfolio model?

I'd been at the company for 25 years in total, and I hadn't really been looking for a new job. I was in a very senior role with a good salary, so if things hadn't changed, I wouldn't have risked that. When a new chairman came into the business, and we didn't see eye to eye, it seemed like a good opportunity for a change.

I was attracted to portfolio work by the variety and the chance to help other businesses—the kind of business that wants a finance director but can't afford one full-time.

I had seen consultants come into our business and I wondered why they always had the CEO's and the chairman's ear. Now I understand: as an outsider, you approach clients with a different mentality. If you are in a fantastic company with a great CEO, you might have the same kind of relationship anyway, but it's much harder to achieve that with the person who signs your paycheque every month and expects loyalty in return. It's easier for a boss to accept a challenge from an outsider who is being paid to challenge the status quo.

The flexibility of life as a portfolio executive was also critical. I have a second business that I run alongside my portfolio work, processing data for a specific segment of the agricultural industry. I'd been interested in it for a long time in the business I was in, but we had never managed to crack it.

Setting out on my own gave me the opportunity to take a step back, take things at my own pace, and develop the business in partnership with an old colleague. It won't make either of us millionaires, but it supplements out income, and we enjoy doing it. There's no way I could have built and run that business when I was a full-time employee. Being a portfolio executive gives me the time and flexibility to work on it and grow it.

What was the hardest part of making the transition?

The hardest thing was the uncertainty. For the first six months, it was difficult not knowing when (or if) work was coming in.

Even though you know that other people have done this and are doing it, you do wonder whether you can make it. Then, when clients finally do start to come on board, you get to feel comfortable at last that it can work.

I'm fortunate that three of my clients are agriculture businesses, and I knew them before joining The FD Centre. Two of them I knew well, and one I had met a couple of times.

What was the turning point?

For me, it was when I brought on a client—a multi-academy trust, which is a group of schools—in September 2016 whose finance director had left two days before the year-end. Because trusts are charities, there is a lot of extra regulation and compliance with their accounts. I got them through the audit with a totally clean report, and even though it was only supposed to be an interim role, I am still there.

Was there anything that made the transition easier?

I was lucky to have the settlement from my old employer. That made those early months bearable, although as the balance went down, of course, things started to get less comfortable.

Getting clients in my industry was helpful simply because of the confidence it gave me at a time when there was enough fear and uncertainty around everything else.

How does it compare to your expectations?

I really didn't know what to expect other than what I needed to earn, and it has matched that expectation.

The interesting thing is that I have a range of clients. With some, I'm very hands-on, getting down into the numbers. At the other extreme, I have a client who only needs me for half-day every two months and I don't have to do any prep work for them. We discuss their plans and I give them ideas for how to move forward, what to do with whichever part of the business they are looking at, and what they need to consider.

What do you most enjoy about the lifestyle?

There's a lot to enjoy. Not answering to a boss, having less stress, being able to go and get my wife some flowers or watch my son's play at school.

There is actually not as much freedom as I thought there would be, because if a client wants you, they get you. Clients are flexible—for example, if I have a client I see on a Tuesday and I need to change it to another day, then most clients would be OK with that—but I wouldn't do that to them every week. Usually, if people know your day is coming up, they'll prepare questions they want to ask you, so it's not fair to keep changing things.

Is there anything you miss about your old career?

I miss the friends I had at my old company. I'd been there for 25 years, so I knew lots of people very well. That said, I have new colleagues now, and I don't really miss much.

I also miss being the fount of all knowledge. When you've been with an organization that long, you know everything about it, and you know the insider's language. When you go into a new business, you're starting from scratch, and you have to learn it all again.

What advice would you give to somebody considering becoming a portfolio executive?

You need to be prepared to deal with the uncertainty, and you need to be patient. There were quite a few people in induction with me in February, and by May they were already saying "I'm not sure this is for me, I haven't had any work yet." You have to hang in there. This is a people business: all you have to do is get in front of people who need you, and if you can get on with them, then you get the gig.

The Work/Care Balancer – Helen Sloman

You have someone else who depends on you for care and support. A full-time position—especially one that matches your level of seniority—would place too many demands on your time and keep you away from home too much, so you need something with time flexibility that you can do locally.

What were you doing before?

I was a product director for an international business. It felt like wading through treacle if you tried to get anything to change, so I managed to engineer my way out and to get paid for the privilege!

Initially, I set up on my own as a freelance marketing director. When I joined The Marketing Centre, I'd been working freelance through my own limited company for about six months. I had got myself out of corporate life, which was great, and I had some private clients, but I was looking to supplement my client list. I did a local search for "marketing director" and "strategy director", and I hit upon The Marketing Centre and applied. The power of Google!

I still have my own limited company servicing my own private clients, and I also work through The Marketing Centre, which gives me access to a larger client pool. And they do business development for me, which was another big attraction.

What did you feel was missing from corporate life?

I wanted more spontaneity and creativity. I wanted to be able to work with a broader cross-section of people. And I wanted to get stuff done quickly, without having to write a big report and go through multiple committees.

What attracted you to this life?

The big draw was the flexibility and freedom. My mother has a long-term illness, so it was great having the flexibility to drop everything and go to look after her if I needed to.

Also, you can choose when and how you work. More importantly, you can choose <u>who</u> you work with.

Yes, you can earn more money in corporate life, but money isn't everything.

What were the hardest aspects of the transition from corporate life?

Surprisingly, a big challenge was the downtime. I wasn't used to having days with nothing booked—in corporate life I was more likely to be over-booked—so I would sit there and think, *What am I going to do?* And I would feel guilty because I was "supposed" to be working.

It helped that I already had my first few clients lined up, so I didn't have that period of uncertainty that many new executives face. I'd been talking about what I was going to do for a while before I started up, so the work was waiting for me. One of my former bosses had taken over a company, and he needed some help, so he became my first client. Along with that, a couple of other people gave me projects as well. I wasn't at full capacity straight away, but it made things a lot easier.

How does it compare to your expectations?

I might sound naïve, but I wasn't quite sure what to expect, so I've been pleasantly surprised.

I struggle with the term *portfolio career* because people don't understand it. When you describe it to them, however, it sounds great to them—especially if they are stuck in a job.

What do you miss most about your old career?

I miss not having gold status with my airline and hotel loyalty programmes—and that's about it!

What advice would you give someone else considering this lifestyle?

The key thing is that you must have experience in your field. If you are fresh out of university, you haven't got the breadth of experience clients are looking for. I do much more than just marketing and communications for my clients. They want a different perspective, an objective viewpoint, and experience.

You have to believe in yourself and be confident in your own ability. People are looking to you for certainty. So, if you feel like you are flying by the seat of your pants or being a fraud, you need to cover it up well. You've got to speak with confidence, and you've got to have gravitas. And that comes from experience.

The Independent Who Wants to be Part of Something – Selina Noton

You've already been successful as an independent portfolio executive, but you value teamwork and being part of something bigger, and you're fed up with the peaks and troughs of working on your own.

What were you doing before?

Before The Marketing Centre, I worked for a major US conglomerate. Working for an American company but being based in the UK, the role required a lot of international travel—at one point I even had a posting in Moscow.

I hadn't hit a glass ceiling. Quite the opposite—promotion was there if I wanted it, and I enjoyed corporate life except for the travel.

What did you feel was missing?

When we had our first child, I realised I didn't want to do so much travel. It was a US company, and if I wanted to progress any further in my career, I was going to have to move to Rhode Island, which neither my husband nor I wanted to do.

So, we moved the family out of the hustle and bustle of London to Suffolk, and the two of us set up our own marketing agency. Unlike most agencies, which focus on project work, we had a number of long-term clients and we were operating as their part-time marketing directors rather than an outsourced creative team.

One day, I was approached on LinkedIn by someone from The Marketing Centre who wanted me to help open up a new region.

What attracted you to this model?

When we set up our own agency, I had independence but I missed the kind of support I was used to in the corporate world.

At the back of my mind, I was also always worried—needlessly—that people wouldn't take me seriously without a big company name on my card. A big part of it was my age: I was still in my 30s, which is younger than most portfolio executives.

When The Marketing Centre first contacted me, I almost deleted the message unread. I thought it might be a scam or a recruitment company harvesting CVs. But, as I read the email, there was something about it that sounded different, so I did some research.

At the time my husband and I had been running our business for eight years, and we had built a strong niche locally servicing clients in construction, engineering, and manufacturing. The Marketing Centre did a lot of work with professional services firms—an industry I'd worked with years before. I like the industry, and I felt it might give me access to some larger organizations. After eight years out of big business, it was quite appealing to go back in— I just didn't want to do it as an employee.

Joining The Marketing Centre gave me the best of both worlds. At last, I had a support structure. I also liked the fact that even though I was self-employed and independent, I was still part of something.

What were the hardest aspects of transition?

When I first left corporate life and set up the agency, the biggest factor was finance, just as it is for many new business owners. We had enough money in place to last 12 months, and that was what we had decided we would allow ourselves. After all, if we couldn't make this work after a year, what kind of marketers were we?

In the end, of course, that's exactly how long it took.

What was the turning point?

The professional trust issue is very personal to me—it's not something that most new executives face—but everyone has something that unsettles them. And it's only when they can get past their something that things will take off for them.

So for me personally, the turning point was when I realised that people were listening and paying attention exactly like they had when I was carrying a big company business card.

What about the transition to being a portfolio executive.

I was lucky that we had money in the bank. I joined The Marketing Centre in August and I didn't get my first client until February. That would have been tough without that financial safety blanket.

If I'd been joining a team that was already up and running, and it took 6 months to get a client, I would have been worried. But, I knew from the outset that I was the first marketing director in a new region and that there was no sales pipeline in place locally.

The local station has a direct train to London, and that is where my first few clients ended up being. I did one or two pieces of work for a different regional director and some short project-based work.

In that first year, I ended up doing work for four separate regional directors, which was good for me because they got to see what I was capable of. It also got me known by people throughout the company rather than just in my local area.

How does it compare to your expectations?

The Marketing Centre typically targets £5M+ turnover businesses, whereas, my private clients were in the £1M to £2M range—companies that tended to need tactical work, things like copywriting and design, rather than strategic advice.

Working with The Marketing Centre has given me access back into the corporate world, which I had been missing because in my own business we worked exclusively with smaller businesses.

I like the tactical level work because it's interesting and I can get my hands dirty, but I also wanted to work at that more strategic level. So I split my time: two or three days each week I work with the Marketing Centre, wearing a suit and attending board meetings to offer strategic insight, then I go and spend a few days with my private clients. I couldn't have that mix and that variety working for a traditional agency or a single corporation.

What do you enjoy most about this lifestyle?

I like being outside all the office politics. When you're working in the same office five days a week, there's a lot of rubbish that goes along with being part of a big company. When you're only there one or two days a week, all of that passes you by.

It's also great that no one has to give me an appraisal anymore, and there is none of the bureaucracy that you find in the corporate world: if I want to take a vacation, I don't have to fill in an annual leave request form.

I don't have to waste time on the red tape and HR that goes with being a manager, either, even though I'm often leading teams for my clients. Instead, I can concentrate on helping those teams, offering best practice advice, and often mentoring individuals to advance their careers.

Finally, I like having lots of different clients and not getting bogged down with any single one.

What do you miss most about your old career?

I don't think I miss anything. The benefits of working for big companies are usually financial: health insurance, pension scheme, company cars, etc. When you work for yourself, you have to take care of those things yourself, but it's worth it!

What advice would you give someone else considering this lifestyle?

Be prepared for the peaks and troughs: there are times when you have five days a week of work, and times when you have none.

And be sure and confident in your own ability to do the job. In this kind of role, the buck stops with you. If you give bad advice, there is no backup like you would have in a big corporation. So, you really need to feel you've done your time in the workplace and learned your craft.

The Career Portfolioer – Michael Meyer

In your mid-30's to mid-40's, you see a portfolio lifestyle as a viable career alternative. While you need money, you value freedom, control and flexibility.

What were you doing before?

I've been an accountant since I was in my 20s, and a CFO for the last thirty years—half of that as an employee and half as a contractor.

Most of my time as a contractor was spent as a sole practitioner, but I joined a regional firm of portfolio CFOs in Atlanta for two years. It was a horrible experience. Their model was "eat what you kill", and I had no support.

I knew it was time to leave when I was in a partner meeting, and one of my colleagues was complaining about how busy he was and that he'd had to turn away two potential clients. I looked around the room, and there were people in there who were less than 20% utilized, but here he was turning down work rather than share it.

I went back to being solo for a while. Then I discovered the CFO Center. Everyone I met was open, friendly, passionate, and helpful. I've never experienced that before to such an extent. So, I signed up, and it's been the best decision I ever made.

I've worked for about three dozen organisations as an employee or a contractor, and The CFO Center is the best one I've ever worked for, from top to bottom and across the board.

I spent the first few months opening up Atlanta, GA until they could recruit a regional director, and then I moved to Richmond, VA to do the same. Despite my earlier experiences, I went in choosing to trust that what I'd been told during recruitment was true.

I also trusted the process. I was going to be me, but I would follow the scripts, do what they said I needed to do, and if they were the real deal, it would all pan out.

It's been a fabulous experience for me. If anything, I've been kicking myself because I started being a contract CFO in 1991 and I never thought about any of this. As I was going through the induction training, I realized that I'd worked out isolated pieces of it for myself over the years, but not all of it, and not consistently.

What attracted you to this model?

Like Colin, I got tired of the frustrations of being in an organisation and the restrictions it puts on you, especially when you have a family. In the corporate world, if I wanted to come in at 10 am, people would get upset because they would leave at 5 pm and they wouldn't see that I was there until 10 pm that night. Even when they found out, it wouldn't matter to them. It was ridiculous. I was expected to be at my desk, whether I needed to be there or not. As a contractor, you have more control over your schedule.

In this business, I've realized you can be part of a team even though you are not getting together regularly. I have a client in California that I visit once a year. In between, though, we have weekly calls on Skype or by phone. I have another client in Atlanta that I've visited twice in several months. With today's technology, you don't need to be physically present, and the kinds of conversation you're having don't require it: they are struggling with an employee, or cash is tight, and they want to know what to do about it. It takes communication and some extra work, but it is worth it.

Another attraction was the variety. I'm easily bored, and I need new challenges. I'm never going to be the kind of person who works for the same company for 20 years. I would be bored stupid. As a portfolio executive, you are constantly getting involved in new situations, and as a regional director everything you do is new: getting involved and helping out, then moving on to the next challenge.

What was the hardest aspect of the transition?

Going from full-time employee to contractor, the big challenge was getting my wife comfortable with the concept and the uncertainty, especially as we had two-year-old twins and a nine-year-old boy at home.

I was an army brat, and our family relocated every two or three years, so I'm very comfortable going into a new environment. I've moved around a lot as an adult—between states, and also between the US and Canada—so I'm not risk-averse, which is different from other CFOs.

What was the turning point?

In the end, what brought my wife round was that I found a client within two weeks. That's fast for this industry, but at the time we were living in Vancouver, and the high-tech sector there was thriving. I knew a lot of people who had worked with me for years then gone on to become CEOs in other companies, so I had a strong network of people who were happy to introduce me to their buddies.

When I moved from Vancouver to Silicon Valley in 1998, it was personal introductions that helped me get things going again. I asked my Vancouver network who they could introduce me to in California and I got 20 names. By the end of my second day, I had a client.

Then, when I moved to Atlanta, I had a client lined up before I even landed. I'm in a group called The Financial Executive Networking Group, so I flew out to Atlanta for an advance trip to explore the market and meet a few of the local members. One of them was a partner with Deloitte and a couple of days after I flew back to Silicon Valley, he called me with a client introduction.

Basically, relationships are critical to this work. Referrals are the easiest way to get started: since joining the CFO Center, 80% of my jobs have come through my network.

How does it compare to your expectations?

Surprisingly, it's better than I thought it would be because the approach and attitudes are universal. We are diligent about being open, passionate, helpful, and friendly, and we get rid of people who don't fit—and that goes for anybody: partners, principals, and clients.

What do you enjoy most about this lifestyle?

The thing I most enjoy about it is being at home. For so many years I did long hours and I was not connected to my family. Now, I can work the hours I choose and work around whatever is going on at home.

The other part is that I like everyone I work with. So much of your work life is spent talking to people, and most of the time you don't like half of them, and you tolerate the other half. With the CFO Center, I can't wait to go to the next conference because I get to meet new people and have great conversations.

What do you miss most about your old career?

I don't miss anything. The part I ended up enjoying there—which was connecting to people—I still have.

What advice would you give someone else considering this lifestyle?

There are two pieces of advice that I give to all my CFO candidates.

First, make sure that your family is on board with the process and the uncertainty that can come with this.

Second, make sure you are comfortable working on your own in an environment where no one reports to you and you don't see people frequently. I'm surprised how many people need to be in an office with people around them.

The Scaleup Enthusiast – Martin Cartwright

You love the variety and interest of working with scaleups—businesses that are beyond startup but are not yet a mature organization—and you get immense satisfaction from helping them grow to the next level

What were you doing before?

I live in Cambridge, UK, which is a great place to be if you are interested in working in the technology sector. After leaving the audit profession for industry, I spent 25 years working in a range of FD and CFO positions in technology companies.

What did you feel was missing?

Joining The FD Centre was ultimately about wanting exciting new challenges. For most part of my career after I moved out of professional practice, my average career span in a job had been four to five years, which is probably not unusual these days.

After the third change, I realised that there was a cycle I would go through every time I moved into a new position.

The first year would be about finding my feet and wondering whether I was out of my depth (I'm sure most readers can relate to that feeling!).

In the second year, I'd figure out all the challenges in the finance and related functions that needed improving, and set in motion a programme to fix them.

The third year would be consolidating what I'd been doing and enjoying it, and looking for more challenges.

By the fourth year, I was starting to feel bored and wondering *what's next?*

I'm not a complacent person. I'm hard-working and conscientious, and I don't like to ever feel complacency setting in. If I'm not being challenged and asked to solve significant problems, I get bored. So, if I made it to the fifth year, I would be getting desperate for new challenges, and I had to find something else.

For many finance professionals, the next step is usually to try to become CEO. I have very strong views on that. If someone is going to be CEO of a technology company, they need to be skilled in either sales, technology, or both. I'm self-aware enough to know that my sales skills are OK, but my technology skills are non-existent, so I've never had any ambitions beyond the finance function.

In SMEs, which is where I've spent most of my career, the finance function is often closer to what I refer to as the "infrastructure" function, covering not just finance, but legal, commercial, HR, contracts, procurement, recruiting, and everything in between.

The one area I never got involved in, despite working in the tech sector, was IT. Working in tech, that was the one thing I didn't need to worry about, and it's still something of a dark art to me.

In 2009, I was the CFO for a high-tech company in Cambridge, and we were just at the end of the banking crisis. Most of our business was with the automotive sector, which had been hit hard by the crisis—private cars are a discretionary spend, and when money is tight, people are much less likely to upgrade their car—so new car sales plummeted, and overnight our opportunities went through the floor.

We were forced to cut 40% of our headcount, which is one of the hardest decisions you'll ever have to make in business, and I decided to put myself on the list of those who would be seeking new opportunities. I'd been there for six years, so I was ready to move anyway. I'd heard about The FD Centre and what they were doing, so I contacted them when I was leaving my old company, and it worked out really well.

What were the hardest aspects of transition?

Working in tech, I'd had several occasions where an old employer had been sold and my shares had been bought out, or I had share options that matured. So, by 2009 I was relatively independent financially.

Most of the people who join us aren't that lucky. My regional director, Paul Dodd, often asks me to speak to potential new portfolio executives to check whether they will be a good fit for the team. Part of the conversation I have with them, though, is about the realities of building this kind of business. It's really hard. You have to be prepared to do a lot of networking, sell yourself, and use your database of contacts from your past career to research opportunities.

And you have to be prepared for the fact that, despite all that hard work, in your first year you'll probably only be 10-20% billable. If you are up for that, then it'll be fine. If you're not, then don't do it.

It takes three to six months to get your first client, six months to get the second, and by the end of the first year, you are probably at 50-60% of capacity.

By month 18, though, things click into place for most people, and suddenly you're bursting at the seams and struggling to keep up.

What's the turning point?

For the first three months, your regional director is getting to know you. However experienced you may be, no matter what your qualifications, and regardless of the big-name companies you've worked for, they don't know what you're capable of, where you can add the most value to clients, or what kind of client best suits you.

That puts them in a difficult position when a new opportunity comes in. The easy answer is to give it to someone who has already proven themselves and is successful. But that person might already have a full client load, so then the RD has to decide whether to take a chance on an unknown quantity.

The turning point for me was that I got a couple of clients in our London region. The local team had a full client load, and some opportunities came up with tech businesses. Cambridge is only a short journey from London, and they asked me to step in.

After that, a number of substantial opportunities suddenly opened up in Cambridge at the same time. From being at 20% capacity seven months in, by the end of year one I was at 80% capacity.

How does it compare to your expectations?

The biggest surprise for me was how different the role of a portfolio CFO is from being an employee CFO. As soon as you step into that role of trusted advisor, the dynamic changes between you, the CEO, and the team you're working with. Chemistry and fitting in with the culture become a lot more important. That took some getting used to, and it was harder because I wasn't there all the time.

What do you enjoy most about this lifestyle?

What I love most is the variety and the flexibility. The variety comes from being with a different client every day. The flexibility means I can work from home every Friday and every other Monday, which I could never have done in a full-time role.

What do you miss most about your old career?

Being from the tech world, I miss being able to share in equity-based compensation schemes. When you're not an executive in the company, you don't get included.

What advice would you give someone else considering this lifestyle?

If you're going to make a success of this, you need to bear a few things in mind.

First, you've got to be comfortable selling yourself, both on your own and working with your regional director and the central marketing team.

Second, you've got to be in a strong enough financial position to withstand a significant drop in your income in the first 12 months.

Third, you will have a lot of variety and a lot of challenges. If that's what you like, then this is the career for you.

The Seasoned Veteran – Geoff Botting

You've been there, seen it, and done it. In your mid-50s to mid-60s, you're a veteran with a vast array of commercial experience over many years and many different economic cycles. You're not ready to retire, but employers just see a pension commitment they don't want to take on.

What were you doing before?

Before joining The FD Centre, I worked in various organisations as their finance director. After working for large publicly listed companies on both sides of the Atlantic, I joined a smaller marketing organisation where I was the finance and operations director for 9 years. While I was there, I grew the business from 12 to 70 staff and grew turnover to four times its size before leaving in 2009.

I started looking for a smaller organization that needed a finance director, but not a whole one. I found one, but in a very short space of time, I ended being responsible for anything that wasn't technical or client related—a combined finance and operations director in all but name. I got involved in everything in the company, from top to bottom, and a lot of the time I wasn't doing FD work. While I did get to work on strategic challenges, general management, and even some acquisitions, I could just as easily find myself having to get someone to unblock a toilet or choosing a stationery supplier.

It wasn't what I'd signed up for, and it wasn't what I wanted to be doing. It also wasn't very cost efficient for the company, and when they went through a rough patch, they couldn't afford to be paying for an FD to work out the right time to order toilet rolls.

I decided it was time to leave, and I realized there must be other companies that needed part of a finance director, but not a whole one. I didn't know how I was going to find them, and I wasn't even totally sure what I would do with them once I'd found them. But I reached out to people I already knew and started a conversation about what I was doing, and where there might be opportunities.

Doing it on my own was difficult: it's hard to find new clients when you're busy delivering to the clients you already have, so it's hard to grow your portfolio.

As it happened, one of my contacts—a managing partner of a local accountancy firm—had recently come across someone from The FD Centre. He saw the similarities between what they were doing and what I was doing and suggested I talk to them. The rest, as they say, is history.

The portfolio executive model suits me well. I choose what I do and how I do it—I only do FD work—and I control my calendar.

What were the hardest aspects of transition?

When I started, it was hard—both financially and emotionally—not knowing when I was next going to get paid. I had a certain amount of money to see me through, but it wasn't infinite. I had a window of time where it wouldn't be an issue if I didn't have a client and I wasn't earning, but I also knew that it would become an issue eventually.

Wondering when the business would take off—or indeed whether it ever would—was emotionally taxing. I addressed it by keeping active, walking the streets, making contacts, and working my network. Most portfolio executives—and I'm no exception—are not natural networkers or marketers of our skills, so that was quite tough.

Also, I lived in a region where very few people had heard of The FD Centre, and I was surprised how few people in my network even understood the concept of a part-time FD. That added to the stress and uncertainty, because I was having to create awareness before I could even create demand.

I got an early client, then I didn't get another one for 6 months. That again was hard, and I started asking myself the questions every new portfolio executive eventually starts asking themselves: would it really work? Would it actually provide me with the earnings and the lifestyle that I wanted? Or was I just heading towards early retirement without realising?

At the same time, I was getting questions at home: "You're sitting in your office all day, making lots of phone calls and seeing lots of people, but you aren't bringing any money in. When are you going to go out to work again?"

Those were six very difficult months for me psychologically.

What was the turning point?

After six months, we got a new regional director who was very proactive and was focused on business development. He spent more time working on leads than his predecessor had, and he started bringing us in at an earlier stage. Suddenly, I got three new clients in rapid succession, and I've never looked back. A couple of those early clients are still with me, and I've always had 3-6 clients on the go since then.

What made the transition easier?

Getting those clients created another big shift. I realized that I could make a big difference to a client in a relatively short space of time. For most of my career, I had been in positions where I could make a difference, but not every day and not so noticeably.

You get one or two clients who—and I'm exaggerating for effect—worship the ground you walk on. You come in, and you have all these tools that they've never seen before that you can bring to their business. So you fix their problem and stop them losing sleep at night, which gives you quite a buzz. To us, we're not doing anything special. It's stuff that we live and breathe. To the client, though, it's magic, because they've never had that before.

That is what makes the transition absolutely positive: when somebody welcomes you through the door and says "I'm so glad you're here. We've got this issue—what do you think about it?" And that sort of thing happens more frequently in that environment than somewhere you've worked for 8 or 10 years, and you are just part of the furniture.

How does it compare to your expectations?

Overall, life as a portfolio executive in The FD Centre has exceeded my expectations. I had spoken to a few people in the business before joining, so I had some idea of what I thought it would be like. The reality, when it came, was what I was expecting, but more of it: the sense of relationship and belonging was deeper, and the difference I made to clients was bigger.

On the other hand, I'd also expected the work to be more relaxed. I thought I would do a day here and a day there. I'd been used to long days in the corporate world, but I—

and my wife especially—had assumed this kind of work would be more 9-to-5, Monday-to-Friday. What actually happens, though, is that the days merge into one another, and into the evenings and weekends.

It's not because I'm a workaholic. It's because it's what the client needs and what the situation requires. When you think about it, though, it makes sense. If you are working somewhere for a day and you won't be back for a couple of weeks or a month, you have to finish what you're doing before you go, or at least leave instructions for someone else to pick it up

By the same token, when you get to a client for your one day a month, you can't spend the first hour sipping coffee and figuring out what you'll do with your time: you have to walk in ready to go. That means you have to spend the evening before getting back up to speed and going through your notes to refresh your mind.

What do you enjoy most about this lifestyle?

The biggest payback is flexibility: doing things in a way and at a time that suit me, with people I want to work with, makes a big difference to me. That flexibility has been wonderful for my family life. I have seen more of my grandchildren than I ever saw of my children when they were growing up.

In my corporate life, I would be gone by the time my children got up, and I was lucky if I got home in time to kiss them goodnight. With my grandchildren, I can pick them up from school, take them out for the day, and do all the things I never got to do with my own children.

I take more time off and holidays than I ever could in a permanent job, and while I tend to work around clients' schedules, I don't have to ask permission to do things the way I would in the corporate world. No one is watching to make sure that you're at your desk by 9 and you don't leave before 5. And if you need to move your day from Thursday to the following Wednesday, for example, most clients won't have a problem that.

You can't treat clients badly, or not turn up when they need you, but you get a lot of leeway.

What do you miss most about your old career?

Nothing. The closest I come is when something happens with a client between visits, and I don't find out about it until the next time I see them, by which time the problem may even have been solved. In the corporate world, I was so closely involved in everything that I found out what was happening very quickly and I often got to be part of the solution.

On the plus side, I've learned to be less of a control freak!

What advice would you give someone else considering this lifestyle?

Be absolutely sure that this is what you really want to do and that you're prepared to do it.

You have to be prepared to leave behind the reliability and security of employment. You have to be entrepreneurial enough to want to do things yourself, but not all the time.

On the surface, it sounds a great life. But, it is not for everybody. Some people prefer the security of a full-time job, the certainty that comes with being in a corporate structure where everyone knows what their role and responsibilities are and what is expected of them.

If you do decide that this is the right path for you, however, then do it, and don't wait. I wish I could have done it earlier in my career, but I needed a few more scars on my back, and I needed broader and deeper experience.

At the same time, this is not something to do early in your career. You need enough experience to empathise with the client, to understand what it's like to wonder whether you'll make payroll next month. If you've been through it, you can be the shoulder to cry on or the sounding board that they need, but you're doing it with the benefit of real experience.

Chapter 4

The Six Virtues

In this chapter, we present six character traits that we have observed in successful portfolio executives. These are the qualities that we are looking for throughout the interview and onboarding process for all Liberti companies. They are not specific to any profession—they apply, rather, to professional advisers..

We've always found it fascinating that some professionals find it easier than others to achieve what they are seeking from this form of working. When you've spoken, as we have, to thousands of professionals seeking a portfolio lifestyle, you develop an intuitive feel for whether people are likely to succeed or not. Codifying that feeling, testing for it, and being certain about it, however, are more elusive.

What we realized is that successful portfolio professionals share a set of six common traits that we call "virtues". They're not competencies, job-related professional skills, or technical skills, but rather behaviours, characteristics, and personal qualities.

As counterintuitive as it may seem, being a truly great CFO, marketing director, or other director in the portfolio world has little to do with whether you are a highly competent professional and everything to do with what kind of person you are.

Of course, building a portfolio requires you to be excellent at what you do, but that is just "table stakes". Clients in this market are typically very demanding, and delivering on your skill set consistently on a part-time basis is challenging: there is no place to hide, and the results of your work—good or bad—are obvious very quickly. So, unless you are in the top quartile of your profession in terms of competency, you are unlikely to go far in this type of work.

In addition to excellent technical skills, however, you also need strong commercial skills, strategic thinking, and an ability to very quickly get to the essence of a client's business and industry.

And finally, you need strong influencing and persuasion skills to get the client in the first place and to be able to provide a quality service and deliver tangible benefits throughout the client relationship.

And yet, we have observed over the years that even when someone has all of the above, it does not guarantee that they will be a top performer. There are aspects of the mindset and behaviours of an executive that are far stronger determinants of success.

Without consciously understanding exactly what those determinants might be, we began to describe people as either "getting it" or "not getting it".

In the early days, we didn't provide specific training on what we did or how. The people who joined us either got it—they intuitively understood our style and performed really well—or they didn't. And if they didn't get it, they struggled, and however hard we trained them on the frameworks and methodologies we were developing to support portfolio working, it was hard work to help them fulfil their aims. For the one who got it, on the other hand, it all seemed much easier.

Later, we switched from talking about "getting it" to "virtues", reflecting our growing recognition that success in this industry is not so much about what you do as your behaviour while doing it. We realized that professionals' behaviours and character traits were much more important to creating success—not just for themselves but for their clients and for us as an organization—than simply being a very capable, highly experienced, technically strong C-suite executive.

And so "virtues" became our shorthand for the high-performing behaviours necessary for professionals to excel in the portfolio world.

When we were planning the research for this book, therefore, we were keen to document the defining virtues of our most successful portfolio executives and also to determine whether these are something you have to be born with, or whether they can be learned and developed.

We believe that, through our research, we have achieved this. We have defined the key virtues that characterise our top performers, and moreover, we have confirmed that these virtues can be nurtured over time through self-awareness, the will to learn, and developing oneself with the benefit of the experience acquired over a period of years.

For anyone interested in this industry, therefore, this is potentially the most exciting chapter in this book. It is possibly also our greatest contribution to the body of knowledge on the future of work, documenting as it does the traits individuals need to excel in the future.

The critical point here is that this is not theory. It is based on empirical data distilled from direct observation, tested over 18 years, and reinforced by interviews with over 30 of our best performers, some of them new to the industry, others with years of experience.

The Virtues

Below we discuss each of the six virtues. We wanted to bring them to life for you so that you can relate to them, see how they apply in the real world, and understand their relevance to the future of work and potentially to you. To do that, we will use illustrations and references from real people in real situations.

It is easy to forget that all the values are intertwined and interdependent. To be truly successful in this space, it is not enough to score well in three out of the six virtues. However Hungry, Networked, and a Learner you may be, your effectiveness can be destroyed if you aren't Humble with it.

Of course, having all six virtues is a big challenge, which explains why so many people struggle when they try to enter this industry alone. That's why being prepared to acknowledge your deficiencies and work on them is critical to your success and enjoyment in this space.

Humble

Building a portfolio lifestyle is all about working in teams. Whether you are freelancing, working a franchise, or operating through the Liberti model, you need to work in and with teams.

As we mentioned earlier, in *Ideal Team Player*, Patrick Lencioni identified humility as the single greatest attribute of a "team player", and our experience and research support this view 100%.

This is not a lifestyle where large egos win the day. Parking your ego at the door on the way into a client can be challenging for a corporate executive entering the portfolio industry, especially when they're working with SME clients.

As we indicated earlier, however, you can't bully and bluster your way through life any more, nor can you rely on brilliant technical skills or political manoeuvring. It doesn't matter how good you were as a corporate executive, or what big-name companies you may have worked for. When you are building a portfolio, it's no longer about you; it's about your client and what you can do for them.

The smart approach is to adapt and fit into the client's team. Doing that across multiple teams and clients, however, isn't easy. Over the years, we've heard too many stories about brilliant executives who are rightly proud of their career history, but they're more interested in talking about themselves than finding out about clients, being curious about their issues, and asking insightful questions and figuring out how they can use their experience to help those clients. They seem to think that because they are brilliant, it's the client who should adapt to the executive's personality.

Often, they come across as authentic in the first meeting with the business owner, but they let themselves down when they are speaking to a receptionist or office worker.

It's a dumb approach.

There's nothing wrong with having confidence in yourself and your skill set. But the best performers in the portfolio space are much more interested in fitting in and figuring out what business issues the client wants solved. They are chameleons, adapting to whatever environment and culture they are in from client to client. At the same time, they are authentic in their approach, building relationships with people in the business whatever level they may be at. And they are personable without being over the top.

There's a story from Colin's early days as a portfolio executive that neatly illustrates how easily things could go south with a client if you don't show humility. He had been introduced to a fast-growing business based in the Cotswolds in the UK—a beautiful part of the English countryside, and not somewhere that you would expect to find a company that cleans drains and sewers and provides cleaning services for industrial plants and oil rigs.

The business was run by two partners who were equal shareholders. Colin had a meeting with one of the partners to discuss how a part-time CFO could help them grow the business to the next level and keep control of the finances along the way. They had been introduced by a bank manager who knew what we could do and could see that the company needed our services.

This was only his second ever meeting with a client, and Colin arrived outside what looked like a small Cotswold stone building in the middle of a farmer's field with some outbuildings and a few large drain-cleaning trucks parked outside. It wasn't what you think of as a "head office", especially compared to the much fancier looking premises he was used to when working for large businesses.

As Colin entered the building, he was greeted by a not-too-friendly-looking dog. It snarled at him slightly, which didn't do anything to calm his nerves. "If only the executives in my previous corporate life could see me now," he thought. "They'd tell me how stupid I'm being, venturing into this portfolio lifestyle and putting myself in this kind of situation."

He didn't even like dogs at the time. But, remembering something his grandmother used to say—that you only have one chance to make a good first impression—he smiled nervously at the dog.

It was an open-plan office, with no reception desk. Politely, Colin asked whether Matthew, the owner he was meeting, was in the office and was told he would be ready for him shortly.

A young lady told "Bess", the not-so-friendly dog, to sit under a desk (which was comforting) and Colin chatted with the ladies in the office for a few minutes while he waited for Matthew. One of the ladies sat in the corner, not joining the conversation, while Bess eyed Colin suspiciously from under the desk.

The conversation with Matthew went well, and at the end of the meeting, they arranged for Colin to return the following week to carry out an initial financial review on the business. He would highlight areas where he felt he could help them, and they'd then decide whether or not to proceed with further work.

Matthew spun around on this chair, pressed a few buttons on his keyboard, and told Colin to pick up the order for the financial review on his way out.

Later, Colin discovered that the original greeting had been an elaborate and well-rehearsed pantomime. The owners of the business had decided long ago that they only wanted to work with people who would "fit in". For them, that meant real people, who were personable, authentic and honest (what we would now refer to as *Humble*). Any potential new supplier who came to the office was deliberately kept waiting in the office with Bess the dog. The ladies in the general office and Bess were the humility test, and the silent lady in the corner was the wife of Nick, Matthew's business partner.

By the time Colin walked into Matthew's office for the first meeting, she had already told him that Colin was someone they could do business with.

Over the next seven years, The CFO Centre helped that drain and sewer cleaning firm achieve some remarkable things, including the sale of over half the business for a multi-million-pound sum. That required high-level strategic skills, strong operational finance delivery, and introducing new relationships to the company that they could not have built on their own.

But it all started with one meeting.

The experience stayed with Colin, and so did the lessons it taught him.

Later, we introduced our own office test known as the Zeus test (after our own beloved boxer dog, Zeus). Over the years, Zeus and the ladies in our office tested many potential portfolio professionals to see whether they were humble enough to work in the portfolio world.

Givers

In his book *Give and Take*, Adam Grant shows that people who give without expecting anything in return are more successful in the longer term. That was something we worked out for ourselves as we attracted more professionals into the portfolio world. What also became apparent, however, was that although many of the professionals who joined us knew the power of being a "giver", very few practised it.

However much we trained them to track "referrals out" as a strong lead indicator of more referrals coming back to the business, professionals (especially in the early stages of their portfolio careers) continued to keep count and to expect other people to go first.

Often in team meetings, when we asked the executives about the relationships they were building with other professional firms, someone would complain that one or other of their relationships was hopeless because they hadn't "given us any work in ages." If we asked that executive what referrals they had made to the firm in question, however, the answer was usually an awkward silence.

It's human nature to count referrals and then return the favour rather than making the first referral, but the professionals who turn that equation on its head by giving first are usually also the ones who get more referrals back.

Caroline Dodds is one of our CFOs. As well as being a portfolio professional, she runs a family—a full-time job in its own right. Alongside her excellent finance skills, however, she is also very humble and a natural giver. As a result, she is always as busy as she wants to be. And she doesn't just generate referrals and business for herself— she is also able to pass on referrals to other members of her regional team.

For Caroline, referrals aren't an effort. She's always looking to add value to her clients. Although fees flow towards her at a level that matches her need, she isn't driven by income but rather by a desire to add value to the client, to make a difference to them, and to change their lives.

Her curiosity and interest in her clients, combined with the experience and connections she has and the connections our business has, make it easy to refer a client to other service providers based on a real understanding of the client's issues and needs. So, referrals come naturally to her, and in her quest to deliver value, the referrals back (and subsequent income flow in her direction) seem equally effortless.

When you think about it, it's common sense. The problem, though, is that common sense isn't always common practice.

Networked

It helps if you come to the portfolio world with a great network. However, you can also build one quickly if you accept that being networked is important. And it is. A great example of this is Rupen Kotecha who worked for The FD Centre in the UK and decided, with his wife and young family, to make a life choice and relocate to Perth, Western Australia. This happened, by happy coincidence, just as we were considering entering the Australian market.

Rupen stepped off a plane in Perth not knowing anyone, with no network or business relationships at all. But he realized that he needed to build a network of business relationships and that it would take a lot of hard work. Most importantly, though, he was prepared to do it.

So Rupen went off and built his network using the methodologies he had learnt in the UK from The FD Centre. He adopted and adapted a number of those methodologies, and worked hard over several years. Gradually, the relationships he built grew first into a portfolio of clients for Rupen and later—as he moved into a team leader and then a CEO role—into portfolios for other CFOs who joined him. In 2016, Rupen was voted one of the top 25 "movers and shakers" in the Western Australia business community.

That's what we mean by "being prepared to get networked." In fact, the way Rupen built the business in Australia was very similar to how Colin built what is now the Liberti family of businesses.

After working for large corporations his entire life, Colin had virtually no local network and initially, he had no idea how he was going to start or build a business. However, he was smart enough to seek advice from a few people that had started service businesses, and they all told him the same thing: unless you have lots of money to pay other people to bring you clients, you have to go out and find them yourself. And the cheapest, most effective way to do that is to build relationships with other business owners and business people who can refer work to you.

Colin's approach, very simply, was to build an initial list of twenty people he thought might be able to help him, either by referring work directly or by introducing him to someone else who would be able to refer business. The list included friends, family, existing business contacts, and old business contacts.

One of those people was Colin's sister, who was the PA to the managing director of a local construction firm. One week, the MD happened to complain to her about the cashflow problems he was having. She asked if he would like to be introduced to someone that might be able to help him with his problem. The MD turned into The FD

Centre's first ever client. And the sequence of activities from that client also created clients number two and number three.

Colin was on his way.

Now, even though most professionals know instinctively that having an established network of relationships can help you enormously when you first enter the portfolio world, the reality is that most people aren't well networked.

People who genuinely believe in building authentic professional networks tend to be more successful in the long term. That doesn't come naturally to most people, however. It takes study, practice, and experience. You need a willingness to get networked and the desire to build that network. There is a lot of information already in the public domain on how to build networks effectively. It's not just a matter of making a few phone calls, and within the Liberti Group, we have developed specific approaches that we know work well in this kind of business and make the task easier.

Relationship

"It's all about the relationship". So says Andy Collier, Joint Managing Director of The FD Centre UK, when describing what it takes to succeed in the portfolio world. Whether you are finding clients, winning them, keeping them, or working with colleagues, you need to focus on people and relationships.

Let me show you what I mean.

Before you can do any work in the portfolio world, you have to find some clients, and those clients don't appear magically from nowhere. One of the main ways to get clients, as we discussed above, is to build your business network. To do this, you need to get out and talk to people, create rapport, and nurture the relationship until the other person feels comfortable referring work to you. And, as we also discussed, being prepared to "give" first to contacts will also help this process. Relationships take time to develop into what you want them to be, however, so being prepared to work at it over time is the smart way to build a continual flow of referrals.

When it comes to meeting the client and selling in your services, it's also crucial to remember the well-known maxim that "people buy from people." Buying decisions are based on emotions rather than data. And emotions are strongly influenced by the relationship between you and the potential client. That's why being a great portfolio professional is not, in itself, usually enough to clinch the deal when it comes to a sales meeting.

A structured sales process can, of course, make a significant difference to your ability to convert. But, if the client doesn't like you—if there's no rapport or sense of relationship—you won't win the business. Providing an excellent service isn't enough: you have to embed yourself in the client's business, which means you need to build relationships with personnel across that business.

Professionals like to think that the quality of their work speaks for them, but in reality, the relationships you have formed are what will do your talking for you. Let's face it, in the portfolio world, you won't be working with a client five days a week—usually, it will be much less—and when you're not there, the client's staff will be talking about you between themselves and to the business owner.

Richard Walker, a long-standing principal in the Liberti Group, always says that a good test of the relationships you have formed is whether or not you are invited to the client's Christmas party. The message is clear: if clients appreciate you being around and they want you to stay with them, they see you as part of the business and you get invited to the Christmas party. But that only happens if you've developed effective relationships with the client.

Finding clients and winning them is one of the hardest things you have to do in the portfolio world, and keeping clients is one of the most effective ways of maintaining your portfolio at the level you want in the long term. So, when you've got a client, you do whatever you can to keep them. Focusing on the client relationship as well as the work you are delivering is a lot easier than losing a client and having to go back into the finding-winning cycle.

Learners

In the future of work, personal success is all about continuous learning—be that the acquisition of new hard or soft skills, or learning from the new situations you experience. Anyone who thinks they are too old or too good to learn anything new is probably not right for this new world of work.

Patrick Murray, who has been the highest fee earner in our UK business for the past three years, is an excellent example of how a commitment to continuous learning is also commercially smart. Patrick always has a full portfolio of clients. He is a full-time portfolio executive, and made a conscious choice to pursue a portfolio career over full-time employment. You might be forgiven for thinking that Patrick's full-on commitment to clients would mean he wouldn't have time to participate in all the learning opportunities that are available to him in Liberti—and there are many, including regional team meetings, national conferences, and special interest learning groups.

The interesting thing, however, is that Patrick attends all of them. That commitment to learning has kept him at the top of his game. He does not rest on his laurels, and he makes time to stay at the top. That's why his clients love him, and that's why he's achieving his aim of being a full-time career portfolio executive.

Hungry (Active)

While this way of working provides a good amount of freedom and flexibility, building and keeping a portfolio is not for the faint-hearted, and our most successful guys are all highly active.

You can't afford to sit and wait for the phone to ring: you have to go out and do the things that are going to grow your business. A strong work ethic, self-motivation, and delivering on promises are critical in this world. Clients like to connect with that type of energy.

When speaking to new portfolio executives, one of the things we always say is that there are three crucial things to remember when working in this industry:

1. Be active,
2. Be active, and
3. Be active.

However, it's also important to remember that being active on the wrong things and doing them the wrong way is a very painful way to be successful. We see this often when executives join us who have previously worked as independents. Some of them are very active but not very effective, and that can have a negative impact on their dreams of entering the portfolio world.

To make sure you get this right, later in the book, we discuss not only the need to be active but also what you need to actively be doing to be successful.

Does This Sound Like You?

If you recognized in yourself the qualities we've just discussed, then you probably have what it takes to succeed in a portfolio career.

If you'd like to explore further, visit
www.TheLibertiGroup.com/getstarted

Chapter 5

Finding Certainty

Working for a diverse range of clients
eliminates a lot of risk, so changing career to
become a portfolio executive can create real
certainty in your life. This chapter shares the
common pitfalls that many executives face in
making the switch, and how to avoid them by
mastering the skills of finding, winning, and
keeping clients.

New portfolio executives coming into the industry typically
have a fixed reserve of money—usually a payout they received
from their last employer, or their savings. That raises two big
concerns for them although, ultimately, both are really about
finding some certainty.

First, they want to know how long that money will keep them
going. Second, they want to know how long it's going to take
them to get up and running.

Neither of those questions is easy to answer, because everyone
is different. How long a certain sum of money will last depends
on the lifestyle you're used to (and the lifestyle you're prepared
to get used to while you get your business off the ground). And
how long it will take you to get established depends—among
other things—on your network, the effort you're willing to put

in, the support structures you have in place, and how quickly you can learn the non-technical skills you'll need. For an independent, the answers depend on so many factors that it's impossible to give a definitive response.

One key statistic to consider is that 90% of new businesses don't survive their first three years—and when you become an independent portfolio executive, you're effectively starting your own business.

Now, you will hopefully earn money in that time. But the problem many independents face is that their business develops in fits and starts. As soon as they get a client, they get diverted away from client acquisition, so they never perfect the skills they need to develop and access the market. Then, a few months later, they're back to looking for a new client and starting from scratch again.

It's that stop-start, feast-famine (or, more often, snack-famine) cycle that eventually drives so many potential portfolio executives back into some sort of paid employment, part-time work, an interim role, or simply working with a small number of clients applying a dumbed down version of their skill set.

They end up running a hobby business with a handful of clients that they've had forever, and hope none of those clients will stop as they have no idea how to bring on anybody else.

The Siren Call of the Regular Pay Cheque

The reason paid employment can seem so alluring when things get tough is that many prospective portfolio executives "grew up" (professionally, at least) with the mindset that employment gives you stability and security.

The reality is, however, that the world of work has changed as technological changes make the market more ambiguous and uncertain. In a world where jobs, companies, and even entire industries can be swept away with little warning, pegging your financial future on a single employer is a much bigger risk than spreading yourself across five companies.

As a result, a portfolio career provides much more income stability and certainty than traditional employment. If you lose a client, then as long as you've learnt the skills to access the market and win clients, you can replace them. And the chances of losing all your clients on the same day are minimal.

Building Speed

Within the Liberti Group, we have found that a new portfolio executive generally takes about twelve months to learn the skills they need to access the market, and get fully proficient. That means you need enough money set aside to see you through at least the first year before you embark on your portfolio journey—and if you're going it alone, you'll probably need a lot more.

One of the reasons why independents need to allow so much longer is that they don't pay enough attention to the Finding activities needed to go to market.

As a new portfolio executive—whether you are working on your own or as part of the Liberti family—the first thing you need to do is build your network in the market—that is your key to ongoing access to the market. Building relationships takes time, and you can't just expect to show up and have people hire you: expect the market to test you. Especially outside of major cities, local markets can be quite cliquey. Business owners already have well-established relationships, and breaking into that can be quite hard if you're the new kid in town.

Delivery skills

When you do find clients, making the transition from employment to high-end service delivery can be overwhelming, especially if you've come from a corporate environment. You're working remotely, serving many clients, and managing multiple relationships within the client. Also, you're not on-site all the time and you're probably dealing with businesses that are very different from what you're used to working with.

So, if you're trying to build a business and learn all these new skills at the same time, you have to make a trade-off between filling your book with clients and making time for skills development. If you don't strike that balance, you'll get incredibly busy but you'll be in an uncomfortable position where you can't afford to lose a single client because you have no idea how to replace them.

That's when the time required—to build the relationships and network that drive long-term success and to acquire the necessary interpersonal skills—becomes a real problem. If you're approaching the market with a very transactional focus—finding clients to serve right now—it can feel like those relational tasks are holding you up and taking you away from your goals.

The truth is, you need to balance speed to market with achieving income stability. Without a solid foundation of relationships and networks, you are setting yourself up for every independent adviser's worst nightmare: the dreaded "feast and famine". So, you need a plan and a purpose to guide how you spend your time. Everyone wants a quick win—to see the things they are doing is working—and you absolutely must go out and win clients early on, but you have to do it in a balanced way in order to 'future proof' your business.

Speeding up the process

Speed to market starts internally. You have to believe 100% that you want to change careers, and you have to be all-in. This is not something you can "have a go at" to see what happens. If you go in with that mindset, then the first time something goes wrong, or someone dangles an alternative opportunity in front of you, you'll get distracted.

So, do your homework before embarking on a career as a portfolio executive. Research the market and the industry fully—you've already made a great start by reading this book—and search deep within yourself. Be sure that it is what you want to do. Because, if you have the belief that it is absolutely the right thing to do, you'll have the 'grit' and purpose to make it happen.

Next, plan how you spend your time so that you balance network building and client finding. Building both types of activity into your plan from the start is the best way to ensure you make time for both.

The reality is, however, that unless you have a marketing "machine" working in the background for you, it's always going to be hard to balance both sets of activities. It was that realization that spurred us to build the ongoing program of marketing activities that Liberti group companies are constantly running behind the scenes for our members. It allows us to take some of the pressure off them and help them to get established faster.

Ask for help

Finally, many portfolio executives are afraid to ask for help—whether from friends and family, peers, clients past and present, or whoever. That fear—or perhaps it's pride—is a key reason why so many newly independent executives fail. Which is a shame, because if you do ask, you'll find people are often more than happy to help.

The way to build your network is not to say, "Who do you know that I can work for?" but rather to ask, "Who do you know that can help me build my network?" It's an easy question to ask that very few people will refuse to answer, and most people are happy to help if they already feel connected to you.

When someone gives you help, always follow up. Remember also to close the loop and let them know afterwards what happened. Don't be "that" person—we've all met them when out networking—who only wants to talk about themselves; the one who asks for help but never lets the people who help them know what they did with their suggestion. That kind of behaviour makes it unlikely that people will offer help a second time.

By the same token, don't be the person who floats around networking events simply to get a business card from every person there. You'll find them in every group: even as they're talking to you, their eyes are already scanning the room looking for their next "mark", and you know they aren't listening.

Staying motivated

There will be times when things get tough. You might have six months when things are going well, and then suddenly it's Christmas or summer, and everything grinds to a halt. After a while, you start to wonder if things will ever pick up again.

When that happens, it's critical that you keep your mood up and keep yourself motivated. It helps if you share some goals with a family member or someone close to you whom you value—you're more likely to achieve goals if you've shared them than if you keep them to yourself. Sharing goals with a significant other also heads off the inevitable question, "So, when are you going to start looking for a job again?" Family support—which we discuss later in the book—can make a huge difference to whether you fail or succeed.

In the end, you need grit and determination. Anything worthwhile takes time, effort, and repetition. And it takes time for the business people you meet to identify opportunities that might help you—they're not sitting with a pile of contacts and suggestions on their desk waiting for you to walk in the door.

Talk to other people in your market who are in the same boat—not necessarily in the same field as you—and get a feel for the level of activity they are maintaining, the rhythm of their workdays and weeks, and when the busy and quiet periods are in the local market. That way, you know what to expect and won't panic.

Know where things are going

One of the surest ways to keep yourself on track is to identify the activities that drive progress, for example:

- number of meetings per day/week/month
- number of referrals requested

- number of referrals received
- number of referrals made to your network.

These are all forward indicators. Think of them as your early warning system: they do not tell you what income you'll make *this* month, but they do tell you what you'll make in *future* months.

To identify what activities you should track, start by recording everything you do and your successes. Look for patterns, and get an understanding of where you, as an individual, work well in a channel. For example, do you find it easier to get clients by picking up the phone and talking to people, or by researching businesses and then approaching them armed with detailed knowledge? Find your strengths and your preferred ways of working, and focus on those so you don't spread yourself too thin.

Building Daily Success Habits

A good way to strengthen your network—this is what Sara used to do—is to build a mind map of everyone you meet and what they are interested in. As they start to introduce you to other people, add information about those new people to your map also.

Once you've mapped out your network, you can look at your map and start connecting people based on their interests. That's how you give to your network—through a conversation, a reminder, another reason to have a conversation. People will love the fact that you've thought of them and given to them, and over time it's human nature that they'll reciprocate and the phone will start ringing.

If you record all of that, keep the faith, and take action consistently, then over a period of time—usually around three months—you will have given enough to your network that the phone should start ringing and opportunities will appear. And if you maintain a steady level of activity in your network, it can become a well-oiled machine that brings you a steady flow of new leads.

None of these activities come naturally to someone who is used to being an employee and perhaps trading off the name and status of their company to get introductions. As an independent, you need to fight for every introduction.

Success in this relies on two things.

First, it has to be something that you do on a daily basis. It can't be something that you try now and then.

Second, you have to follow up. Often, we're afraid to follow up in case we are rejected. We worry that people will feel that we are bothering them. Often, however, people are busy and forget, so they're grateful if you follow up.

The value of external support

All of this becomes much easier if you have external support in place—something that isn't your own personal resources, business, or network. That's what draws many independent executives to organizations like the Liberti group which provide access to staff and resources an individual couldn't hope to match. It also means you won't have to keep reinventing the wheel to create business processes that were probably taken care of by your old employer.

Now, as founders of Liberti, you may assume that means we're now going to say, "So join us."

We're not.

Every year, Liberti group companies receive thousands of approaches from executives who want to join us, and we reject 99% of them because either they don't have the right level of experience or they're not a good fit with our culture.

What we can tell you, without any bias, is what to look for in any organization you are thinking about joining. One of the big advantages of being part of a larger organization is that you are no longer just selling yourself—something many professionals find hard—but rather a proven solution with proof and continuity. So, there are two critical things to consider.

First, make sure they have a track record. You want to join something that is already working well and is at a later stage than your fledgeling business.

Second, look for an organization where you are part of a true team. One where you can tap into the collective knowledge and experience, and there are client-finding activities going on while you work without relying on you.

Taking advantage of downtime

Inevitably during this early stage of your business, you will find yourself with time when you are not serving clients—more, probably, than you would want.

This is time that could be gainfully used making new connections and strengthening existing relationships. And yet, many professionals struggle to do that. Even with the support system of the organization behind them, there are some executives in Liberti companies who let fear get in the way of going out to build relationships.

That's a terrible waste. Particularly if you spend that time sitting in the office either finding busywork (redesigning your business card) or fretting over how you'll find the next client. It's imperative instead to spend as much time as possible in the marketplace building relationships.

Building skills

For most professionals, learning and development is something that is firmly in their comfort zone, so it's tempting to sign up for more training as a way to avoid going out into the market—rushing from one conference or workshop to the next.

Building skills is important (it is, after all, what we are selling) so you still need to make time for it—*after* you've dedicated enough time to building your network. Beware of signing up for more and more technical training courses, however. Assuming that your technical knowledge and experience are at the right level to go out into the market on your own, your learning time would be better spent acquiring skills you don't have than sharpening the skills you already have.

It's tempting, when starting out, to assume that the reason you're not getting clients is that you don't have enough of the "right" technical skills. That if you can just find the one that is in demand, your business will suddenly take off. The reality is, the skills you are most likely lacking are relationship building and selling.

That's where the Virtues we discussed earlier come into play. It's not by chance that the Virtues focus on soft skills over technical skills. Those are the skills that will help you get and keep clients.

Don't Try to Do Everything

One trap that independent executives fall into easily is to feel that they have to do everything for their client. For example, a new portfolio CFO may see some bookkeeping tasks that need to be done. Rather than reach out to their team (if they have one) or their network (if they've built one), they add the work to their own task list.

The problem is that they will be charging CFO rates for bookkeeping tasks, and within one or two billing cycles they lose the client who feels, quite rightly, that they are being over-charged.

It would be better to bring in someone at the right level and oversee the work. Even though the client may be paying the same amount in total, it's easier to swallow split over two people than one. And by bringing in another professional, the CFO is showing that they are putting the client's needs ahead of their own, which builds trust.

The importance of Sales and Marketing

If you're not getting traction in the market, then the problem is either with your sales or your marketing: one (or both) of those is failing for you.

Ultimately, there's a simple formula underpinning any business:

No marketing = No sales = no money =
no freedom/flexibility/variety

Moreover,

No method (no marketing machine) = no stability =
time to go out and get a job

Catchy film slogans aside, just because you build it, doesn't mean they will come.

But I'm making sales, do I need to do this?

We've often come across executives who have been going for a while and seem to be doing well, then one day they suddenly start struggling, and before you know it, they're gone. Usually, those are executives who were well connected in their corporate life and who have been living off their old network.

The problem, if they have many years of experience behind them, is that their network ages with them. People who used to be in a position to help them move on, go freelance themselves, or retire, and eventually their network dwindles away. However, because they haven't had to do any business-building up to that point, building a new network seems even more daunting than it might have. Surprisingly, that's often when those experienced executives start to look for a home in an organization like Liberti.

Finding Skills

It's time to get into the nuts and bolts of marketing, and we'll start with what we call "finding skills". These are activities designed to identify businesses with needs—an opportunity for you to help them—and to set up meetings to talk about those needs.

You need to have a solid set of channels—routes to market—and you need at least two: being dependent on a single way to get clients is a guaranteed recipe for business failure. At the same time, you must avoid spreading yourself too thin by trying to leverage too many channels at the same time. Each channel you use is going to require an investment of both time and money, and it's easy to run out of both if you try to do too many things. You'll also struggle to do any of those channels justice.

Exactly which channels you should be developing is something you need to figure out for yourself. It could be your "little black book", your partners, Google ads, or something else. Find the ones that suit your temperament and your strengths, as we said earlier, and concentrate on those.

Free Channels

Initially, you probably won't have a lot of money for marketing, so look for "free" ways to promote yourself. I've put free in quotes because there is no such thing as truly free marketing: if there isn't a financial cost for something, you'll end up paying for it in time and effort instead—but that's fine in the early stages of your business when you're probably cash poor but time rich.

Existing connections

The first obvious route to market—at least while you build new relationships—is to make full use of your existing relationships: family, friends, social and business connections, colleagues etc.. Within Liberti, we call this "street marketing".

Start by reviewing all the connections you've had in your career and categorizing them as either "hot", "warm", or "cool" based on how helpful an introduction by them is likely to be. A hot connection, for example, is probably someone you know very well, who is going to be able to make a strong introduction, and who is well-connected and respected so that the introduction will carry weight.

Don't be too proud or underestimate the benefit of family and friends in this regard. Remember the story from earlier: the first piece of work The CFO Centre generated was from Colin's sister Joan, who was the personal assistant to the managing director of a local construction firm.

Our experience in Liberti shows that these regional channels based on personal relationships convert much better than anything else, simply because when you find an opportunity, there is a trusted third party vouching for your credibility.

The problem is, these sorts of introduction are high quality but low volume.

In contrast, the new connections you make through market outreach will be higher volume, but you don't have a strong relationship or a track record with that person, so they'll convert much less readily.

This "street marketing" is where most professionals come unstuck, because it's completely unfamiliar to them. Moreover, if they've been on the receiving end of it, it was usually badly done, because the person asking for an introduction didn't know how to approach it, so their reference experiences haven't been great. That's why a lot of the initial training we do with new Liberti group executives is about how to have structured conversations, and especially how to approach people in prior relationships that you may not have spoken to in a while.

The process starts with your little black book—the people you won't mind picking up the phone to because you have an existing relationship with them. Pick 20 names from the list, sit down, pick up the phone, and start dialling. When you start the conversation, don't make it all about you; be interested in them. "Hello, I haven't spoken to you for ages. I just wondered what you are up to."

People love talking about themselves, so that will last a while and give you lots of information about what they're interested in. Eventually, they'll ask "What about you?" and that's the opportunity to bring up the subject of your new business, reposition yourself, and say what you're interested in, which should then lead to them offering help. If they don't, you can ask: remember, you're not asking for business, you're just asking for help to build a network.

Look for at least two introductions from each person in your network, because that is going to maintain a good level of activity. And make sure they are personal introductions—you're not collecting scraps of paper with strangers' email addresses.

Networking

The other side of street marketing is going to local business events and networking groups. You need to work out who is operating in the market, which are the best events to go to, and who goes to them.

You should also be looking in local newspapers and business magazines and seeing what businesses are going through some sort of change that could indicate an opportunity for you. In the early days of the first Liberti group business, the CFO Centre, we used to do that all the time. We would see organizations making a large investment like a new factory, or PR about a new initiative or an award they'd won, and we would use it as an excuse to get in touch.

When you call, get the boss's name by chatting nicely to the receptionist, and then write a very targeted and benefits-driven note directly to the owner.

It's always much better to pick businesses in sectors that you are familiar with. As business owners ourselves, we know that when someone shows an interest on that level and can relate to our industry in some way, it's flattering, and it's much easier to start a conversation.

You can achieve a lot through local networking. There's a certain amount you can do from your desk, but the more people you talk to the better: hiding away to do research has its place, but at some point, you do need to go out and talk to people.

Client referrals

The single best way to get clients, however, comes once you've got a client and you can start to generate client referrals. The best businesses can turn four clients into ten just by asking the clients they already have for referrals.

It's as easy as doing a good piece of work and then spotting the opportunity to ask for a referral: "Who else do you know that would like this type of intervention, where I could really add some value like I have for you?"

One of the most powerful referrals—and one that very few professionals think of—is to a supplier. If your client's supplier has a problem and your client wants to secure their supply chain, then referring you is a win-win.

The key thing when asking for client referrals is to ensure that you plant the seed up front, when you first win that piece of business. Tell them that you grow your business by referral: "When I've done a good job, can we have a conversation about that? Because I'm sure you know other businesses that need help."

The first time you ask a client for a referral can be quite scary. In effect, you're asking "Am I doing any good?" and hoping that the answer is yes. The very first time Sara asked a client for a referral, his reaction was "I've been waiting for you to ask. I wondered when you'd get around to it! I know exactly who you can work with. I've told her all about you and I'd love to get her in here so you can meet her next time you're in." He arranged everything, from agreeing the date and time down to organizing the meeting room.

Asking for a referral was a tremendously pleasurable experience and very easy because his business had benefitted from us working together and he wanted to share that.

And remember: many business owners have built their business that way, so there is no shame in it.

Referrals from Partners

Another very powerful—and lucrative—set of relationships to build is with businesses that are potential referral partners. The relationships a referral partner has with their own clients is hugely valuable to them, so they aren't just going to refer them to anyone. You will need to have to put time and effort into building the relationship up front.

Look for partners that are a close match for you both commercially and culturally.

Commercially, those are companies that "get" you, that are in the same marketplace, and that have a good relationship with their client.

Of course, everyone says they have a good relationship with their client, so what does that really mean? It means they are having the right conversations at the right level, emotionally and strategically. For example, Libertines are excellent referrers because our key relationships are all at the CXO level, we are emotionally connected to our clients, we are at the heart of our clients' strategy, and we see our clients on a weekly or monthly basis. There aren't that many partners in the market that are as closely integrated with their clients and have the depth of relationship that our executives have.

Events

Running events is a well-established model in the consulting and advisory industry, but that doesn't make it an easy option. Filling a room with leads is hard, and if you're struggling to find clients one at a time, you'll probably struggle to put ten potential clients in a room. That said, events are a low-cost channel to market.

The key thing is, they don't have to be *your* events. You don't have to be the one putting people in the room. Find events that are already happening in your market and piggy-back on them. Show the organizer that you have expert knowledge that will add value to the event, build a relationship with them, and get an invitation to speak.

When you're at the front of the room, you get exposure and you're positioned as an expert. Just make sure you have some sort of call to action, and follow up.

Paid Channels

So far, we've discussed channels that have no financial cost—although they do cost you time and energy. Now lets look at channels that do require a financial investment. Use the free channels to build your business and add value, then start investing into the other channels to add more value and to gain clients from those channels later on.

Email marketing

Email is an important channel. 40% of our new business in Liberti group companies comes through this. The key is to build your own list. Now, we don't know where you are or what your local email laws are, so please check what is and isn't permitted in your country. In most jurisdictions, however, a personal email from you to a named individual whose email address you've found through your own research is unlikely to raise too many eyebrows.

Start by thinking about how far you are happy to travel to a client. For example, you may decide you will only look at businesses within an hour's drive of home.

1) Search online for businesses less than an hour's drive from home.
2) Look at their website and whittle the list down to the ones you would want to work with.
3) Research them and their industry thoroughly.
4) Approach the owner/CEO with a very personal email which talks about some of the issues you've identified they might have from your research

5) Discuss what you might be able to do to help them and spark some interest that way.

That will generally get some sort of response direct from the CEO.

As soon as you can, however, you need to start building a permission-based email list, which brings us to the next channel.

Pay-per-click

We started to use pay-per-click very early on. The secret to making this work is to identify the keywords people are using in searches related to their needs. Of course, the challenge for a portfolio executive is that you have to have all your other marketing in place first in order to make your pay-per-click work, because no one will be searching for part-time directors if they don't know what they are or even that they exist.

Also, it's very easy to spend a lot of money on pay-per-click and get no result if you are sending them to something that doesn't work at the other end, for example running an ad to your home page. Visitors are not going to come to your website and be so blown away by your qualifications and your choice of colours and images that they feel compelled to call you immediately.

When you're paying for traffic, it's critical that you send it to a page that has a call to action that converts. Make them fill in a form so that you can follow up with them. And do that follow up immediately. If someone has searched for you and taken time to answer your questions, you know they have a burning need. If you don't follow up within seconds, however, they'll just go to the next search result.

That brings us back to email marketing. Pay-per-click is a great way to build a list for email marketing: send traffic to a page where they can request valuable information (not a newsletter!) and get them to agree to keep receiving information from you.

SEO

SEO—search engine optimization—is getting harder. First, there's just so much competition. Second, search engines keep changing the rules.

So, it's a challenge for an individual to rank highly for specific search terms. It's much easier for established businesses to get there because their efforts are backed by PR investment, lots of online activity, and plenty of high-quality backlinks. They are also more likely to catch up faster when Google moves the goal posts, as it regularly does.

Moreover, with SEO you are effectively borrowing traffic from Google (and maybe other search engines), and it's hard to control the flow of that traffic to your website. When you need it, you may not get it, and when you get busy, you may not be able to stop it. With pay-per-click, in contrast, when you need more traffic, you raise your budget, and when you need things to calm down, you lower it.

So, SEO is a channel best left to larger businesses. It's simply too hard for one individual or a startup to do well and monetize effectively.

Social Media

For Liberti group businesses, social media means LinkedIn. That is where we build our professional relationships. At the same time, we are doing more with Facebook and tracking our results. Twitter, on the other hand, has not generated a lot of clients for us.

Your business and your market, however, may be different. You need to figure out where your clients are on social media, what they're doing there, and what they're looking for. Does that sound familiar? It's exactly what you should be doing in real-world networking.

Many people use social media as a broadcast channel, which is the equivalent of going to a networking event and talking about yourself all the time. You can get far more traction by adding value through joining groups and conversations. If you can find the right groups on social media that have the right conversations and then add value, that will pull people towards you.

What's working for us on LinkedIn

Let's look at the LinkedIn strategy for The CFO Centre as an example—bearing in mind that it doesn't matter what's working for us; you need to find what works for you, in your market, with your clients.

We start by connecting with the owners of businesses in a local market. Often, that is enough to make them look at our offering, and they may realize that they need us.

In addition, all our executives' profiles are connected and they are constantly sharing content—client testimonials, thought leadership articles, and discussions—to position us as thought leaders in the CFO space, which again attracts leads as well as building our brand.

A major benefit of this approach is that communicating through LinkedIn helps us to stay on the right side of anti-spam laws. Once we are connected to someone personally, we can start a conversation freely. That makes LinkedIn very valuable to us.

Your website

Another critical asset is our website. Many experts spend a lot of time, effort, and money creating a site that is little more than an online brochure and doesn't convert. If you're spending money to get visitors to your site—for example with pay-per-click advertising—your website needs to be compelling and encourage people to communicate with you, whether it's through a signup form, a live chat, a download, or whatever.

Want to see an example?

Visit www.theFDCentre.co.uk or www.theCFOCenter.com to see how we do it in our CFO business.

You'll find the web address of other Liberti group companies at the end of this book.

Assessment marketing

People love to find out about themselves, and business owners love to find out about their own business. And if you can show someone where they stand relative to their peers, it's even more powerful. That's why, for example, many print magazines regularly include quizzes and self-assessments.

For us, assessment marketing—in the form of the F-Score—is a major source of leads, and our prospects get real value from knowing how they are doing in relation to the marketplace. However, although assessment marketing is a great tool for your website, remember that you will still need to drive web traffic to it.

Partners and Assessment Marketing: Another powerful way to use assessment marketing is to allow your partners to use it in their newsletters. Partners are always looking for new content, and you can agree to share results with them—though you'll need to disclose this to visitors.

Using Assessments at Events: You can also build events around your assessment, and get attendees to complete the assessment and benchmark themselves against other people in the room.

Other Places to Use Your Assessment: Your assessment can be used to qualify leads before you even speak to them. Put links to it everywhere you can think of: on the back of your business card, in email signatures, in your brochures, on postcards, in your print ads, etc. For us, one of the major sources of traffic to our F-Score is a call to action in Colin's first book, *Scale Up*.

You can also ask all your leads and opportunities to complete the assessment in advance of your first meeting with them.

PR and Advertising

We always get business from PR and advertising. As PR has moved online, however, it's getting harder to be heard or seen among all the competing content.

PR can be paid—by hiring a PR agency—or free. The key is frequency: you need to keep up a flow of stories and news in order to get a good response rate. The big success factor for us in the early days was building relationships with the journalists.

Ask your client what business magazines and publications they read and target those to build a relationship with a journalist. Those relationships also pay off when it comes to running ads. Every publication has a publishing deadline. As that deadline approaches, you can pick up advertising space at "distressed" rates, and it's easier to get those when you have a friendly contact on the inside.

Book

It's getting harder to stand out in professional services. More and more people are starting their own business as consultants, coaches, and advisers. And the situation is made even tougher because, however good your qualifications and experience are, your competitors usually come from very similar backgrounds, and truthfully, most prospects don't understand—and don't care about—the difference between professional bodies and their certifications. They don't care whether you call yourself a "chartered professional X" or a "licensed certified X" or any other combination of titles. It's meaningless to them.

If you don't find a way to clearly differentiate yourself from those competitors, you'll end up as a commodity and clients will find their own way to choose, which usually ends up being around rates.

For Liberti group companies, our differentiation comes from the scale of the organization behind every member (1,000 executives covering 7 disciplines in 16 countries), proven processes, and the breadth and depth of our relationships with firms in other industries. That provides a lot of reassurance and credibility that makes us virtually unique in any meaningful comparison a potential client wants to make.

As a sole practitioner, it can be harder to communicate that level of credibility, experience, and authority to clients, but one of the most powerful tools you can create is to write your own book. When journalists and TV producers are looking for someone to interview for their opinion about something in the news, who do they ask? The person who wrote a book on the subject. Faced with two very similar advisers, who will a prospect choose, the one who gave them a business card at the start of the meeting, or the one who handed them a copy of their book and signed it?

Even for us, a book is an incredibly powerful marketing tool—the fact that you're reading this book shows that it got your attention. In fact, this is our second book, and we have a third in the pipeline. That should tell you something.

Follow-through and follow-up

Most professionals fail at selling simply because they don't talk to their prospects enough times. There's a lot of research about how many meetings are needed before a sale is made. While exact ratios vary from study to study, what we have found is that regular, polite and persistent follow-up does lead to more sales.

That's why email marketing works so well; it allows you to automate your follow-up and keep in touch when your competitors have given up.

Over the years, we have tested the follow up process and its frequency many times. We have found that most professionals don't bother to follow-up more than once and yet our experience is that busy entrepreneurs with many demands on their time are very grateful when we politely keep the dialogue open and keep in touch. We have numerous examples of business owners responding to us after the fifth or sixth attempt to connect with them. Often they are very apologetic about not having responded sooner, but at the same time very aware that this is the very reason they need our help.

Standing Out in a Sea of Sameness

We mentioned above the difficulty of differentiating yourself in an increasingly crowded market. If you have extensive experience in a specific sector or function, that will give you an edge initially, but it can also restrict your market. One of our CFOs was a partner at KPMG before becoming a CFO in industry. As a partner, he had specialized in corporate finance, and even though he had worked full time as a CFO, when he set up in business on his own he was still seen in his local market as "the corporate finance guy." He wanted to become more of a generalist, but every opportunity that came to him was in corporate finance.

It was only when he joined the CFO Centre that he was finally able to reposition himself and break out of the box others had put him into.

There's a dilemma facing executives embarking on a portfolio career. If you want to work independently, the way to stand out is to double down on whatever your perceived specialism is. Even though it will mean fewer prospects, the ones who do come to you will come knowing that you're the right person for them.

If you're trying to break free of that professional straitjacket, however, then the beauty of working for a company like The CFO Centre, or The Marketing

Centre, or any of the other Liberti companies is that because you're seen as part of a larger business, your personal expertise is taken as perfect for the job; the assumption is that you've been pre-vetted and you are ready for the job, whatever your functional background.

Winning Skills

So far, we've focused on "finding" skills: the activities necessary to identify opportunities and get in front of potential clients. Of course, getting a meeting with someone who needs your help is not the same as getting them to sign on the dotted line. For that, you need "Winning" skills: the ability to turn an opportunity into a paying client.

Route to market matters

When it comes to closing a deal, your route to market—how they came across you—can be a major influencer. It will determine how you are positioned when they meet you, how much—if anything—they know about you, and whether they are a "cold" lead, a "warm" lead, or a "hot" lead. That, in turn, will determine how you conduct yourself in the meeting, what you need to cover, and how long it will take to close them: our experience is that a warm lead can be closed in as little as 14 days, while a cold lead may take 45 days or longer.

One of the most valuable things you can do to help your sales is to train referral partners fully on how to make a proper introduction. Professionals starting out on their own rarely give this the attention it deserves. As a result, even though their contacts want to make a referral they don't know what words to use, so they either never make the referral, or they do it badly and make the sale harder.

This was a lesson Colin learned very early on, courtesy of a local partner in a national accounting firm. While Colin had started building a good relationship with the partner in question and had referred clients to him, he hadn't done a particularly good job of briefing the partner about what would be a good client for The FD Centre. As a result, all the accounting firm's impossible cases started to land on Colin's desk.

While part-time FDs do work for troubled companies, these particular companies also had very difficult owners who wanted everything done for nothing. Colin soon learnt that being very clear with a referral partner on what constitutes a great client is an important skill for building a part-time executive business.

Help your referrers by sharing how you want to be positioned, and role-play the introduction so it comes naturally to them and they can say exactly the right things to enable it to happen.

Fear gets in the way

Many executives have an almost irrational fear of the sales conversation. In large part, it's really a fear of rejection. Especially when you're selling yourself rather than a firm, every sales meeting can feel like you're asking for validation of you as a person and as a professional; like you're asking the other person "Am I good enough?"

When that happens, it can be hard to differentiate rejection of the offer—which you probably didn't express very well—from rejection of you, which is not necessarily what is going on.

If you've never been trained in how to sell, you need to go on a sales training course. You need to learn how to ask questions and dig deeper. And you need to get used to the idea that the first answer is not usually the real answer, and "no" usually just means "you haven't given me a good enough reason to say *Yes*."

High-quality sales conversations

A high-quality sales conversation is a structured conversation with a qualified lead to identify the real need in that business. The critical stage of that meeting is what we call the "fact find". While you'll uncover symptoms—things that are happening in the business that the owner wishes weren't—far more important are the emotions the owner is feeling about those symptoms. That's what they really want you to solve. And if you can show that you can take the pain away by resolving the issue, then you'll win the work. You just have to give them confidence that this is the kind of thing you do on a regular basis.

Another critical aspect of the meeting is qualification, especially when it comes to pricing. Too much time is wasted by professionals in sales meetings that should never have happened because they are trying to sell a Mercedes to someone who is shopping for a Ford Fiesta.

By the same token, many professionals assume that they have to be the cheapest competitor in the market because people won't hire them otherwise. Then you find yourself trying to sell a Nissan Micra to someone who wants a Porsche. All that does is undermine your credibility and destroy their confidence—the buyer will simply assume you're not good enough to charge a "proper" fee.

If you do your research up front, that kind of mismatch shouldn't happen.

The billing cycle you can't get out of

One of the biggest dangers for new executives is that in the early days you're desperate to get work and you undercharge just to get the client.

The problem is, it's easy to put yourself in a low price bracket, but much harder to get out of it. A better way to achieve the same result is to pitch initially for a small, self-contained piece of work to show that you can give a great experience. Then, once you've reassured the client that they made a great choice, pitch for a larger engagement, with a correspondingly larger price tag.

In fact, that's how Colin won his second ever piece of work. An initial two-day assignment to review the workings of the finance function at an environmental services business led to a second piece of work to review asset funding of capital expenditure, which in turn led to Colin being retained as part-time finance director. Over the years, that single client generated over £1 million in fees for The FD Centre, and when it came time to sell the business, it was The FD Centre that they turned to for support.

The Proposal

Starting with a small piece of work can also help you to avoid the need for a written proposal. When a prospect asks you for a proposal, it's usually for one of two reasons.

1) They still have some objections that you haven't handled.
2) They want to show it to someone else for validation. Again, that might be because they still have doubts, but equally, it may simply be the way their business works.

Proposals take time to produce, and often there will be one thing that you don't say in quite the right way and it puts up a barrier. So, before you run off to create a proposal, try to find out why they want it, and whether you can move ahead without one.

Instead use that small, self-contained piece of work as a proof of concept and to show the value you can deliver. That minimizes the risk to the client, and it's much easier for you to show them in the sales meeting that the value you can create is worth the risk.

Proof

That small piece of work also gives you the best opportunity to provide proof of what you can do. Testimonials and referrals are great, but there is always the doubt on the prospect's mind that "it worked for them, but will it work for me?" When you deliver value directly to the client, however, they can see and feel that it works for them.

The virtues that will help you win

The secret to closing the deal is good communications skills and emotional intelligence: the ability to read the body language and feel the energy in the relationship. Within the Liberti Group companies we use a model called Communication Styles, which categorizes people into three styles: Thinkers, Feelers, and Knowers.

For example, Knowers want to receive information succinctly. They want you to get to the point and give them the headlines—they typically use a lot of bullet points when they write, and their speech can sometimes feel like bullet points too. If you're presenting to a Knower, then spending too long in the sales meeting and painstakingly going through all the detail will drive them nuts. And it will probably lose you the sale.

So, you have to adapt your style to fit the person you're meeting while having enough emotional intelligence to know your own approach. If you've plugged your skills gap and worked out what your communication style is, adapting to other styles will give you a big step forward.

Giving

Many professionals worry about giving too much away in a sales meeting, in particular that if they tell the client what they should do, they will try to do it themselves. They forget that clients could probably work it out for themselves anyway, and if they could do it themselves, they would have done it already, and there'd be no need for a meeting.

Never be afraid to give in a meeting. The more value you give, the more the client will trust you and come to believe in your capabilities, and therefore the more likely it is that they will hire you.

Make it about them

In the sales meeting, be humble. Even though you are the expert, the meeting is not about you and what you can do. It's about them and what you can do *for them*. That requires the confidence to hold your space, knowing that your experience speaks for itself. Avoid the temptation to try to impress with your track record. They don't care. They just want to know whether they get on with you and how you can help them to solve the problem they have. The rest will come later.

Keeping

One of the great aspects of the advisory industry is that there is no predetermined end to the relationship: as long as you can keep delivering value to your clients, they will continue to seek your advice—we have clients who have kept their portfolio executive even after being bought out or bringing in venture capitalists.

Once you've found an opportunity and turned them into a paying client, you need to keep hold of them. The "churn and burn" model—a constant stream of short one-off assignments—isn't sustainable in this line of business. Retaining clients for the long term allows you to build your reputation and deliver true value to the client.

It's also more fulfilling for you professionally, as you get to accompany the entrepreneur on their journey and deliver their goals and aspirations. You get to see the fruits of your labour, go through the different stages of the lifecycle with your client, expand your skill set by facing new challenges, and build your distribution network.

Losing Clients

The financial cliff that faces many new portfolio executives makes it tempting to take whatever work comes up: you see a potential client and how much they need your expertise, and you think, "Great! I can do all that for them in a short space of time." There's a balance to be struck, however, between time and money: how much of your time they can use, and how much money they can afford to pay you.

If you bill too much early in the relationship, the client may decide it would be more cost-effective to hire a full-time employee. If you give too much of your time, on the other hand, you become an employee in all but name, and you can't build your own business. So, if you do a substantial piece of work up front that is going to take a lot of your time, you have to make them understand that that level of time and effort is not continuous—that it will drop down—and check that they are happy with that.

Too often, an inexperienced portfolio executive starting with a new client will look at all the work that needs to be done and assume that they have to do it all themselves. If they're running low on cash, it becomes even more tempting. The problem is, they're putting their own needs ahead of the client, doing work that should be done by a hired assistant, and charging too much for it. Eventually, the client figures out what's happening, trust breaks down, and the executive is out.

Now, imagine if, instead, the executive goes to the client and says, "This work needs to be done. I'll help you find more junior staff to do it, and I'll manage them." Immediately, they're building trust and laying the foundation of a long-term relationship by focusing on the lifetime value of the client rather than the next billing cycle.

Communication is Critical

Often, in finance, marketing, IT, and similar areas, there is a lot of groundwork to be done, and a long lead time before that work starts to pay off. In those situations, communication—positioning your work six-months ahead and managing expectations about the timing of results—becomes critical in building a long-term relationship. You'll need to create a clear work plan of what needs to be done, then check in regularly and itemise everything you've delivered. This becomes even more important when you're doing strategic work that isn't directly revenue generating.

When you're working with a client that isn't used to working with people at a strategic, C-suite level, it's in your interest to deliver some quick wins early on to reassure the client. However, they then come to expect those sorts of wins all the time, which can lead to awkward conversations when your focus switches to long-term business improvement and future growth.

And if there are no quick wins and everything is going to be painful and take months to deliver a benefit then you're in trouble. Especially if—as is sometimes the case—things will feel like they're getting worse before they get better.

Manage Up and Across, Not Just Down

Experts are often so keen to deliver that they put their head down and get stuck into the content of the engagement. In every piece of work you do, you need to pay attention to managing the client as well as managing your tasks and team members. That doesn't just mean the business owner or the person who hired you: you have to identify all the stakeholders involved and deliver value across the board.

It's not just about doing great work

Delivering great work, communicating well, and managing up, down, and across the organization are all prerequisites for the portfolio executive. However, the often-missing magic ingredient is trust: specifically creating trust with clients based on your own character.

The key to maintaining your portfolio over time is to deliver on promises, build rapport, and become part of your client's business so they can't imagine life without you. It's also a good idea to get involved in any social activities at the organization. Richard Walker, one of our long-standing finance directors in the UK insists that a good indicator of whether the client will keep you for the long term is whether you get invited to the Christmas party.

Applying the Virtues to Keeping

Learner

Being a Learner helps greatly when it comes to keeping the clients you've got. You have to be curious. However experienced you are, and however many qualifications you have, you can't afford to sit in an ivory tower. You have to get down into the detail of the client: how does the organization really work, and where can you add the most value?

Humility

In the context of keeping a client, humility is putting the client and their needs first and having open conversations. It's also about the intent behind what you do. It's tempting, when you first go in, to start to fix things in order just to look good. Always ask yourself: Am I doing this because it's what the client needs or simply because I need to be seen to be doing something? Or because it's what I know to do, and I do this with all my clients?

Networking

Clients aren't just hiring you, even if that's what they think they are doing. They are also getting access to your relationships. That network is an invaluable resource that you can bring to bear in client assignments as a shortcut to getting to the right people.

Conclusion

Marketing guru Dan Kennedy says that as an entrepreneur, your business is not about "doing" whatever your skill set is; it's about marketing those skills. Ultimately, the key driver of your future success is your ability to create continuous access to the market. If you don't have that, you don't have a business; you have a job.

Chapter 6

Support Mechanisms

No substantial business has ever been built by one person acting alone. Even the great entrepreneurs of today, are all backed by a strong team. In the context of your small portfolio executive business, you need structures in place to plug skills gaps, provide moral support and motivation, and ultimately to allow you to scale the business beyond yourself.

Many professionals come to the world of portfolio executives from an environment where they had a team to support them: peers to confer with, junior staff to help with delivery, administrators to keep things running smoothly. They're not used to working on their own and being the person who does everything, from invoicing to making the tea to closing the client.

Indeed, harsh as it sounds, they may not even be aware of all the different tasks that need to be done because they have always had someone to do things for them. They've never had to do their own accounting, diary setting, expense management, marketing, or any of the other hundreds of things that happen in the background at every business. And if they did, it was probably the part of their work they least liked. The part that got in the way of doing the "real" work.

Of course, you can always hire an assistant to do all those things for you now, but that takes money, which is probably the one thing you don't have enough of when you're starting out. So, you need to learn how to do those things and build them into your routine right from the start.

A word of warning

Of course, not all professionals shy away from the support tasks. Some throw themselves into it with gusto. Often, however, they do it because as much as they may hate bookkeeping, they hate the thought of picking up the phone to a stranger even more. So, they look for filing that needs doing, or they obsess over the logo and text for their business card: anything, so long as they can avoid going out into the market and building relationships.

It's not just about admin

In your business, you need two types of team, and therefore two types of support.

1. admin support
2. peer support

When you're starting out, it's really useful to surround yourself with like-minded, similarly skilled part-time directors, and go to market as a team instead of an individual. There are many fewer teams out there than independents, so a multi-person team immediately stands out.

Even though you may have similar skill sets, you'll each bring different experiences and different focus and specialisms. As a result, working as a team makes you more attractive because you can offer a broader range of services, cover a wider geographical area, support clients in more ways, and bring more knowledge and experience to bear in any client engagement.

For the team, it also means you can be more active in the marketplace to find clients, you can be present in more channels, and it's more fun and supportive. Having others around you on the same journey is good for morale; it will keep your spirits lifted when things aren't going well.

Human beings need to "belong". Often, our professional identity is grounded in the teams and organizations we are part of, so quitting your old employer can leave you feeling adrift and without that identity. Being part of a team can help restore your identity and rebuild that missing sense of belonging; of being part of something bigger than just you.

Finally, of course, being in business on your own can feel incredibly lonely—especially if you need to bounce ideas off someone. A team takes away that isolation.

> For many executives in Liberti Group companies, one of the biggest benefits of the team environment is that they can always get an answer to a client question, even when it's outside of their experience. It gives them real comfort and confidence knowing that they're not going to be caught out, they're never going to be out of their depth, and there is always someone with the right experience that they can turn to.
>
> And sometimes it's just good that they have access to someone who can reassure them that they're doing the right thing.
>
> Many of them tried to build their business on their own before joining us, so they know what it feels like when that peer support isn't there.

What makes it difficult to build a team?

Of course, building a team from scratch—whether it's an admin team or a team of peers—isn't straightforward. When it comes to admin support, there are two big challenges.

The first is deciding which areas of support to prioritize and spend money on. Should you hire a personal assistant first? A bookkeeper? Or would you be better off hiring someone to handle marketing while you close and deliver? There is no set answer, because every business—and every executive—is different. You need to become aware of what the big pain points are for you. It's also about leverage and return on investment. And before you start to spend money on support, you have to be making money. Otherwise, you're going to burn through your startup cash reserves and savings twice as fast.

The second challenge, which appears as soon as you've decided what you're going to invest in, is finding the right people.

In the early days, when you are building up your business, you probably won't need fulltime staff. In many ways, in fact, you're in the same situation as your clients: too big to survive without someone, but too small to justify hiring someone fulltime. In that situation, virtual assistants, who are usually sharing their time across multiple clients, are invaluable.

If you're hiring a virtual assistant, I suggest you hire someone who is part of a virtual team—there are companies out there who do that—because working with an individual creates too many risks. If your assistant falls ill or goes on vacation and they're working alone, you have no support during their absence. And if they decide to shut down the business or take a full-time job, you're left with no support at all. With a team, you have the reassurance that, in those situations, there are other people behind your assistant who can pick up and carry on without interruption.

Of course, what I've just said should give you a clue why clients find it so much more appealing to work with you if you're part of a team too.

Attracting director-level peers to join you in servicing clients brings its own challenges, not least the need to find like-minded individuals. It's not easy to find people of the right calibre who want to do things in a similar way, see the same opportunity, fit the culture you want to build, and want to build the business how you want to build it. Of course, those are the same challenges facing any organization that wants to grow, but they feel much harder when you're facing them alone.

What Support Looks Like

I said above that many professionals don't initially understand all the different forms of support they may need, so it might be useful to give you an example by discussing how Liberti Group companies support their executives.

Our support is structured around implementation of what we could call the Liberti model—the proven methodology we've developed for building a portfolio business. When an executive joins the CFO Centre, for example, they get extensive support with admin, IT, and marketing. As a result, they:

- don't have to set up their own website.
- don't have to think about a company name and logo. They just get their business cards—although they do need to set up a personal service company through which to trade.
- don't have to go out and find support for invoicing and accounts.
- can use our existing networks in their local area to start building relationships and get introductions to the right people.
- benefit from regional and national marketing activities across multiple channels.
- get taught our proven approach to finding, winning, and keeping clients.
- have a pre-built team of peers, with regular team meetings and conferences.
- get regular learning and development, including both business development and professional skills training.

Most Liberti Group companies have also developed their own branded methodologies and other intellectual property for their executives to use in servicing their clients.

Indeed, the only "admin" work most of our executives have to do is to manage their diary and expenses. They could hire an executive assistant to handle those, but most don't bother. It also means that the professionals joining a Liberti Group company don't suffer the pressure most independent professionals do as their business grows, to move away from their professional skill set and become people managers.

Identifying the Right Team Members

Given the difficulty of finding the right professional peers to add to your team, how can you check that someone is a good fit before you let them in?

Again, we have spent 18 years finding out what works and what doesn't. So, I'll describe the Liberti recruitment process, and you can work aspects of our approach into how you find your team.

For us, it's important that potential recruits not only have the right professional skills, but also that they have the right attitude and that they fit in with existing team members. Recruitment in all the Liberti businesses is a four-step process, culminating in what we call "the barbecue test" (which is so important you'll find it has its own section later in the book!).

Over the years, we've built up a very comprehensive profile of the attitudes and competencies that we know work for us. If you're doing this for yourself, you won't initially know what those are for your business, so you're going to have to rely much more on gut instinct.

There will be times when you either spend too long and get too far down the line with people who aren't suitable, or you may even bring people into the business that you later regret and end up putting too much energy into trying to make things work. When that happens, take it as a learning opportunity, and take those lessons forward with you to the next set of recruitment discussions.

One of the critical characteristics you should be looking for, however, is someone who takes responsibility for creating their own portfolio within the structure you're trying to create. Some people will come to you expecting everything to be done for them, including finding the leads and closing the sale, so that they just have to deliver. That's the mindset of an employee, not a portfolio executive, and you can't afford to bring those people in.

You Don't Have to Build a Team

Of course, there is no rule that says you must build a team around you. Instead of setting up a formal team or partnership, you might decide instead to build informal ties to other professionals so that if any of you find yourself with too much work (it does happen!), you have trusted partners that you can bring in, either as a referral or under your own banner.

While this is a useful halfway house between being a sole practitioner and building a full-blown firm, it does need to be managed carefully: over time, if you don't pass along enough work, or you don't nurture the relationships enough, partners will lose interest and look for new relationships.

Alternatively, you may prefer to keep things to just you, service your clients, and have an "easy" life. There are distinct advantages to going solo. When you work alone, you have total control over what you do, who you speak to, and how you market yourself. You only have to support yourself, and you're not responsible for what happens to anyone else. Fewer than one in every hundred new businesses ever break through £1 million revenue, which is still a relatively small business. It's enough to sustain one person but doesn't stretch far if you're having to share it with three or four partners and paying support staff.

By staying on your own, you also avoid all the problems of managing people and dealing with different personalities—exactly the things many professionals leave corporate life to avoid.

The disadvantages, of course, are that you have no support. If something happens to you, or even if you just want to take some time off, everything stops. You're also more susceptible to "feast and famine": as soon as you get busy, it's easy to let your sales and marketing tasks slide—or you simply don't have time to do it because you're caught up in delivery for the clients you already have. You have to be rigorous in carving out time to keep selling, even as you get busy.

Of course, if you do keep selling when you're busy, you create another problem, which is that you generate clients that you can't service. That's where relationships with other professionals—whether in a formal partnership or as a loose association—come into their own.

Joining an existing team

The final option open to you, of course, is to join an established team rather than trying to build your own. Joining an organization that is already up and running has many advantages. If it is successful, it will have a bank of market and professional knowledge, routes to market that are working and bringing in new business, and effective admin and marketing support. It's a machine that will keep running whether you're with clients, sleeping, under the weather, or taking a well-earned vacation. Importantly, you're not having to reinvent the wheel, and you're not having to learn entire skill sets that, to most professionals, are not only unfamiliar but usually uncomfortable, if not downright scary.

Against that, of course, you have to balance the loss of some of the independence that probably attracted you to this workstyle in the first place, and the risk that you may not fit into the culture of that business. You have to find an organization with values that resonate with your own and the business model has to suit you—in particular, the time commitment expected and the remuneration model.

Family Support

Professional support is all well and good, but the biggest single determinant of whether or not a new portfolio executive will stay the course is often the support they get at home. It's so important that all Liberti group companies have built it into their recruitment. Joining us has to be a joint decision, and one of the first questions we ask prospective members is "have you discussed this at home with your partner/spouse/family?"

Becoming a portfolio executive is, in effect, a new career that requires many new skills. There will be days when things aren't going your way, when everything feels much harder than you'd expected, and when you'll start to second guess yourself. On those 'down' days, you need people to lean on, to remind you why you made the decision, and to point out all the things that are working. The worst case scenario is when your significant other isn't on board. When you're wavering, the last thing you need is someone at home who is also questioning why things aren't going well and when you're going to get a "real" job.

In Liberti businesses, we encourage applicants' partners to talk to the partners of executives already in the business. A big part of the problem is the uncertainty, so it can be very reassuring to speak with someone who has been down the same path, who can say "yes, that happened to me, but we stuck at it and now here we are..."

Of course, the impacts on family life aren't all negative. Becoming a portfolio executive gives you more choice and more control over your agenda. Yes, clients will have expectations that you need to meet, and there will be marketing activities to carry out, but on the whole, you control when and how you do those. You're not tied to 9-to-5. You don't have to go to the same office every day. You can carve out time for things that are important to you—things that you might not have had the chance to do in a corporate environment—like attending your children's activities, supporting your partner, or doing a hobby that's important to you.

Maintaining boundaries

There is a dark side to that freedom. It's easy for the lines between work and non-work to get blurred when you work from home.

When your work computer is in your house and you're constantly walking past it, it's tempting to sit down and check emails, work on a report, or whatever, and before you know it you're working out of hours.

Nicky Milward, one of our marketing directors in The Marketing Centre, is balancing being the mother of three sons with running a successful port-folio business. She confided in me that as she got busier, she realized she wasn't getting the flexibility she wanted from this career. She felt constant pressure to service her clients, and there was always something to be done in the evenings.

The key to working through those challenges has been discipline, including forcing herself to take one day off every week for herself. That is something over which she has total control, and it is down to her to make it happen.

Professional Support

As well as peers to support you in delivery, there is value in being around other like-minded professionals who aren't necessarily working with you. Within Liberti group companies, executives are encouraged to network not only with the members of their direct local team, but also members of other teams around the country and in the corresponding companies in other countries—people who won't necessarily help them with delivery or with finding clients but can be valuable as sounding boards. Because everyone knows that they will be in the position of needing help at some point, they are very responsive when a request comes in, whether it's for information, contacts, or something else.

If you're not in a Liberti business, you're not alone, of course. It may be hard to find a community that is as close-knit and responsive as what we have built in the Liberti companies, but you can join industry associations—every profession has at least one—that provide networking opportunities and often have online forums where you can at least ask for help.

Learning and Development

One of the biggest gaps professionals encounter as they move into working for themselves is the opportunities for personal and professional development that they enjoyed in their corporate life.

Clients hire a C-level resource because they are looking for reassurance. They need to know that the person they are hiring is at the top of their game, and is up to date with the latest trends, developments, and regulations in their industry. As an independent, it's up to you to make sure that you're meeting those needs for yourself or that you can get up to speed very quickly. That's a big task and represents an equally big investment. You may not always have to pay for that training, but it's time when you're not delivering (and therefore not earning).

Again, I'll explain what we do in Liberti group so that you can copy the strategy in your own business. Because it's so important, we've built personal and professional development into the fibre of Liberti group companies. We've formed special interest groups for individuals to build their expertise in specific areas, and they can feed that expertise back and share it with their teams.

A lot of our development, however, comes through our network of referral partners—what we refer to as our distribution relationships. We have distribution partners in many industries, and they train our executives free of charge as part of their relationship with us. For example, when GDPR came into effect in May 2018, our portfolio executives understood exactly what impact it would have on their clients not only from a legal standpoint, but also IT and Marketing. The executives paid nothing for that training—they just had to get themselves to the training venues.

For our partners, the payback comes in the form of improved referrals. When our executives understand what a partner firm does and how they can help our clients, it is easier for them to identify opportunities for making an introduction.

Conclusion

The key to success in business is to have support structures around you, and the easiest way to do that is to build (or join) a team. Whether you're working alone or as part of an organization like Liberti, you're part of an ecosystem. You need to understand all the elements of that ecosystem and invest in it—whether in time or money. Think of it as an investment in your future that you will be able to draw on and extract value from.

Ultimately, trying to do things on your own, without any sort of team or support system around you, is setting yourself up for failure. And it's unnecessary, because you live in a world where you are surrounded by all the resources you need. You just have to map those resources and create a plan for making the most of them.

Chapter 7

Is This for You?

Working as a portfolio executive is not just about being technically competent. You're launching a new career, and that requires new skills: marketing, selling, administration, retaining clients for the long-term, client service, and other business skills.

When you're working with SMEs rather than big corporations, you're often the first senior executive they've had apart from the business owner. The business owner is usually a specialist—in marketing, technology, or whatever—but probably has gaps in management skills. As a result, you can add massive value to the client simply by bringing general business skills alongside your core specialism.

That's why we don't accept executives into Liberti companies who have only worked in an advisory capacity—in an accounting or consulting practice. We look for people who have both industry experience and general business skills. To succeed as a portfolio executive, you have to have been on the front lines and accumulated wider business skills that will be beneficial to your clients.

Assessing your skills

So, how do you know if you've got what it takes? Obviously, it's hard to get twenty years of experience in judging and assessing executives overnight.

However, start by looking at the competition—other independents in your area, smaller teams of executives, and teams from larger businesses like Liberti. Talk to them and score their capabilities and yours to see where your gaps are (and theirs).

In Liberti, we aim to fill those gaps for our team members and teach them the skills they need. If you're doing this on your own, you'll have to find your own ways to address the gaps. That might be through training, or you may have to partner with other executives with complementary skills to your own.

The Generalist Trap

Despite what I said above about the need to have broad business skills, it's a mistake to go to market as a generalist. If you try to position yourself as a general business solution, you're in competition with every business coach and independent consultant in your market. Worse, it's a very vague offer. So, even though smaller businesses, in particular, need it, it's difficult for potential clients to understand and even harder to buy. That's why Liberti businesses go to market as specialists—in finance, IT, marketing, etc.—even though the group as a whole could provide clients with an end-to-end solution for almost any business problem.

Once you've got a client, it's much easier to start a conversation about other ways you could help them, especially once you're delivering value and getting results.

What this isn't

Many new portfolio executives come into the industry as a way of filling time while they look for a permanent role. That's the wrong attitude. This is a career change. It's the destination, not a route to another role. If you treat your clients as projects rather than a long-term relationship, then your mind is going to be on your future role, rather than the needs of the client. You'll focus on fixing the immediate problem, without necessarily considering the client's longer term direction and needs.

Meanwhile, if the client is taking you on as a part-time (rather than temporary) executive, they clearly have an expectation that you are in it for the long haul. It's unfair to them if, six months into the engagement, you tell them that you've found something better.

Functional Skills

We've spoken about the importance of broader business skills. At the same time, of course, you do need to have the qualifications and experience for your field. It might be tempting for a marketing manager, say, to call themselves a portfolio CMO and get a client as a way to get C-level experience before looking for a permanent role. And many clients don't understand the difference between a marketing manager and a marketing director well enough to realize what is happening. They'd only find out when their new hire was out of their depth—by which time it's too late.

In Liberti companies, we see it as our duty to educate the market. We spend a lot of time educating prospects and clients about what the C-level role entails, and what experience and qualifications they should be looking for.

By the same token, no-one can join a Liberti company unless they have the skills and experience of a C-suite director. We provide opportunities to continuously improve those, to keep up to date on technical developments, and to acquire the business-building skills to be a part-time portfolio director, but we are not there to train anyone in the basics of their profession, or to put them in a position where they could let a client down.

The biggest requirement

The single most important requirement for a portfolio executive, however, is that you must enjoy working with small businesses. If you don't—if you miss the corporate environment—then this is not the career for you.

Life in an SME can be a culture shock if you have always worked in a large company. In a corporate role, there's always someone to take care of details, and a lot of things get swept up by support functions. SMEs are much less formal, and you can't avoid getting involved in the nitty-gritty of day-to-day life.

You'll find yourself having to roll up your sleeves and do things that wouldn't have been part of your role in your old life, and you can't afford to be precious about it. More often than not, the buck stops with you: you're the one who will go to the workshop, the one who sends out the flyers. You may even have to do your own photocopying! Initially, you may even find yourself doing technical work that you would expect to hand off to a junior, at least until you are able to hire someone.

The Portfolio Executive as Leader

Even though an SME usually has a leader—the owner-entrepreneur—it's useful if you've sat in their shoes. If you have, then you sit with them as their peer. That experience might come from having run a business, but it might equally be from running a business unit within a larger organization, or helping a wife, husband or life partner who run their own business. The key is that you understand what it's like to wonder how you'll make payroll, or feeling the weight of responsibility that every entrepreneur feels. That understanding gives you empathy and enables you to build a deeper relationship with your client.

As a portfolio executive, you are called on to show different kinds of leadership on a daily basis. First, you need to be a leader to your clients. As their C-level resource and expert, they are looking to you to lead your function. That is the role they have hired you for. Second, you are also the leader of your own business. It is you who creates the vision and strategy of what that business will be and what it will become. Even if the business is just you, you need to know what you stand for, why you are doing this, and what your values are. That, in turn, will allow you to find the clients who match that vision and will fulfil you. It also becomes part of what differentiates you from competitors, at least for the "right" clients.

Discovering your Purpose

As an independent, you need to get clear on your personal "why" for choosing this lifestyle, this way of working, and what you deliver. Articulating that will attract clients who connect with that broader purpose. That means that your why can't be "to pay the mortgage": it has to be about the change you want to create in the market.

It's easy to say that you should know your purpose, but many professionals struggle to find theirs. Your purpose exists at the intersection of what interests you, what you are able to do, and what you are motivated to do. Ultimately, it's what you are passionate about. It's what makes you want to get out of bed in the morning (rather than having to). And it's always there, not just 9 to 5.

> One of our marketing directors, Helen Sloman, works with a group of care homes. She connects deeply with that specific client because her mother has dementia and she is caring for her. So, she identified closely with the client's aim to be the most trusted partner in their sector.
>
> There's a real chemistry between them, and Helen truly wants to help the client achieve that vision.
>
> And because the client's vision and Helen's are so aligned, her work is far more fulfilling. It stops being just another "job".

Vision

If your Purpose represents your "Why", your Vision is your "What"—the future you are trying to create. It is the North Star that guides you and gives you direction.

Some professionals wonder whether clients really care about their purpose and vision. It's true that in many cases, clients engage with you initially because they need a problem fixed. Then they stay with you because of your competence. After a while, however, as the relationship deepens, it becomes about your character. That's when they become interested in you as an individual, why you are doing things, and what you're trying to achieve.

However, there are also clients for whom your Purpose and Vision are major reasons for hiring you. They are attracted to what you are trying to achieve and why, and they buy into that.

Why Vision Matters

People want—and need—meaning in their lives. They need to know that they are making a real difference and contributing; that they matter.

In their corporate life, many professionals are used to turning up to work in the morning, doing their job, and then going home at the end of the day. If they're lucky, they work for a company that has a vision they can buy into, and their fulfilment comes vicariously through helping the organization achieve that vision. It doesn't occur to them to have a vision for themselves.

As a portfolio executive, however, you need to create that for yourself. Your Purpose and Vision give meaning to the work you do. Without them, you don't know where you're heading, or what progress you're making. And without direction—without a goal to work towards—or any sense of achievement or progression, the work eventually becomes empty and unfulfilling. It starts to feel like you're in a job rather than running your own business.

Sara's Vision and Purpose

The vision I have is to be one of the creators of the global portfolio executive industry. Liberti is about creating a whole new way of working—a new future of work based on team-based portfolio lifestyles for professionals—that changes our lives and the lives of our clients forever.

Portfolio working in teams means that we can de-risk our careers forever. We learn lifelong skills to be able to access the market when we need to. We work together in teams so that we are always supported and can deliver the power and knowledge of many to our clients. We have a real focus of 'giving' to build sustainable, mutual relationships and a sense of real meaning in our work.

My purpose is to create relationships that make a real difference and deliver more freedom and success to our team members, clients and wider community.

Everywhere I go, I see professionals in every country and every area of expertise seeking freedom and wanting to experience flexibility, variety, and control over their lives. They want to be able to be themselves and to balance their work with their friends, families and hobbies.

I also meet entrepreneurs in every country who are looking to grow their business and need access to someone who can provide a strategic, commercial, C-suite skill set, along with emotional support and understanding, but because of the size and scale of their organisation, they only need them part-time.

I do what I do because I want other professionals to experience what I've experienced through being able to work this way and I want business owners to realize their aspirations through our support. I love the flexibility it gives, the variety, and above all the freedom. The possibility that more people can experience this as a sustainable way of working and living—but in a team-based environment rather than having to do it alone—blows me away.

Culture

It's easy to assume that culture is something only big corporations need to worry about. But even as an independent, your business has a culture. At its simplest, it is "the way we do things around here." It manifests in your behaviours, which are driven by your values.

In the same way, every client you work with also has a culture, and that culture will determine whether you work with them, and for how long. It's far easier to add value to a client when your cultures match: they are easier to work with, you'll enjoy being there more, and—more importantly—they are more likely to respect and follow your advice.

So, you need to be clear on the culture you're building, and what you're looking for culturally in clients.

Why This Might Not Be for You

By now, you may be wondering whether this is the right career choice for you. Let's look at some of the factors than can be a turn off for some potential portfolio executives.

The time to get going

First, as we've discussed already in this book, is the length of time that it takes to get the business up and running. It takes a year to build a portfolio successfully and feel financially secure. Even at that point, you won't have recouped the money you invested to get that far and the lost revenue in the early months. And that's for someone in a Liberti business with access to our existing relationships and our business-building activities. If you're doing this on your own, of course, it can take even longer.

The first six months are exciting and worrying at the same time. It's exciting because you're doing something new and you have hope and self-belief. But it's also worrying because you can't always see immediately whether things are working, and it can feel like you're not making progress.

When Sara was going through that initial period, she would often call Colin—who had already been through it—for support, fretting that she only had one or two clients and couldn't see where the next one was coming from. Colin's advice was something we still give to all our new executives: "Keep the faith. Keep doing the activities."

Everyone goes through that phase. It's especially hard if you don't have support around you, if you have financial worries and you can see the cliff edge getting nearer, and if you get no support or understanding from your family.

That is when many new executives are tempted to give up, particularly if another opportunity comes along—which they will. Sometimes, you'll be out networking and building a profile in your local market, and you'll find something that could make all the pain and uncertainty disappear. And if you're not really comfortable with the uncertainty, you're having doubts about the business, and you're not seeing signs that it's working, it's very easy to jump back into a permanent role even though that's what you wanted to get away from in the first place.

Another danger—one which will extend the time it takes you to get going—is over-analysis. Many new executives, for example, are afraid to contact the people in their address book. They go through the list second-guessing themselves, and coming up with reasons not to call each person: *someone else has probably already spoken to this person, that person won't need/want to hire me, it's been too long since I spoke to this one.*

Insecurity

The next potential turn-off is the lack of income and job security. The start-up period, where you don't have your old permanent role but you don't yet have your portfolio up and running, can be stressful. As the time stretches out, you can start to wonder if you've made a mistake and this is going to become one of those unexplained gaps on your CV that future employers will hate. That piles on the pressure to cut the "experiment" short and find a traditional job.

When Sara started her business, she worried about what her old colleagues would think. They were all now in senior roles in large corporations, and there she was, struggling to build her portfolio in an industry most people didn't even realize existed, and working with very small businesses. Despite the lack of validation, however—which was mostly in her own head—she kept at it, and the rest—as they say—is history.

Back then, Sara dreaded being asked "So, what are you doing with yourself these days?" Today, however, all those people still trapped in their corporate jobs are more likely to think *That sounds a lot better than where I am. I have to get on the train at 7 am each morning, and I come back at 7 o'clock at night. I stand on the same spot on the platform every day with the same people, and it feels like I'm just a slave.*

Feast and Famine

Another "feature" of the portfolio lifestyle that many executives struggle with is *feast and famine*: the pattern of alternating periods where you're either so busy you can't do anything else or you're struggling to pay the bills.

It can happen because when you start out you have nothing, so you take clients that need more than a day or two each week. Instead of being a portfolio executive, you end up as an interim director, working all but full-time.

Alternatively, you may find clients who really do only need a day of your time, but you decide you want to over-deliver, so they'll be delighted and refer you to everyone they know. So, you start going in more often, and after a while it becomes the norm.

However it happens, the time commitment leaves you with no time to find other clients until the engagement finishes. After you finish, of course, you're into a period where you have no work—and no money—again. And you can't enjoy the time off because you're worried where the next client will come from.

Running a business rather than filling a role

As a portfolio executive, you need to understand that you're no longer just filling a technical role, as you probably were in your corporate life: you are running a business. Most portfolio executives struggle with that because they have no experience of it and they've never developed those skills.

Being on your own

For many new portfolio executives, the biggest turn-off is being alone. When you're only seeing a client a few times a month, there isn't much scope for socialising with people there. You can make it happen if you really want, but it will take effort. At the same time, as an independent, you don't have a team of your own to socialise with. So, it's easy to feel lonely, and you don't have anyone to bounce ideas off, to check that what you are doing is right, or to turn to for answers when you don't know. That can be a scary position to be in for someone who has built their career on being the expert.

Overwhelm

As a portfolio executive, there's a lot to be done—especially if your client is in a bad way and looking to you for a quick solution. That can quickly become overwhelming if it highlights gaps in your experience and you don't have support. You start to second-guess yourself because you don't know what to tackle first, and you end up doing nothing.

Character and the Barbecue test

The barbecue test is how we decide who we will or won't bring into Liberti companies. It's a simple model that you can apply in your own business when talking to potential partners, team members, and even clients.

Metaphorically, we are not looking for the kind of person who wants to stand in the corner and talk to one or two people: we want someone who will jump in and start cooking sausages on the barbecue; someone who is very comfortable building relationships with everyone there.

In practice, it means we are looking for someone who fits our values of *open, progressive,* and *passionate*; they know they are not the finished article so they actively want to build new skills; they want to build long-term relationships, and they have what we refer to internally as "grit", which we define as perseverance, passion and purpose. Richard Walker, one of the executives you read about earlier in the book, has a saying: "You don't have to be very good at this to get started. You just have to have belief and keep going. Then you learn how to get good at it."

The barbecue test encompasses three areas: being self-aware, socially-aware, and team-aware.

Someone who is **self-aware** knows how they show up; they are conscious of their level of motivation and how they interact with others. It's also about having emotional intelligence and leaving their ego at the door; being adaptable; and striving to continually build their skill set, improve, and invest in their own personal development.

Socially aware is about being a giver and well-networked; building long-term, authentic relationships without needing to take from them immediately, entrepreneurial; and having empathy with business owners rather than being judgmental.

Team aware is about having a collaborative approach and understanding that the whole is greater than the sum of the parts—that the more you collaborate, the more you gain.

Together, these are the qualities you need to succeed as a portfolio professional and deal with all the complexity, ambiguity, uncertainty and volatility you'll encounter in the world out there.

Conclusion

Building a new business is always a risky undertaking and building a portfolio of clients can test your ability to handle risk to its limits. The exact nature and extent of the risks you face will depend on your individual circumstances, so you will need to work out what those risks are for you and how to mitigate them.

For some, the risk is financial: do you have enough money to see you through the early months? For others, it's about the fear of wasting time: will this fail and set you back in your career? Others worry about reputational risk: how will you be seen by your peers?

Ultimately, it is your attitude to risk in general, and to the specific risks that you perceive, that determine whether this is the right career for you.

Chapter 8

Preparing for a Portfolio Career

In this chapter we cover all of the things you
need to have in place before you launch.

If you've got this far, then we assume that you're mentally
prepared for the lack of income stability and the fact that
it'll take some time. Also, that you have your support
mechanisms in place and the "grit" to keep going. And
that the benefits of the portfolio lifestyle outweigh the
turnoffs.

Funding for the build

Becoming a portfolio executive is not a decision you make
lightly or overnight. You need to plan for it while you're
still in a full-time role and start building your war chest.
How much you'll need depends on the lifestyle you're ac-
customed to, and what you (and your family) are prepared
to put up with throughout the build phase. As a minimum, you need at least one year's money in hand so that

you can give it enough time without feeling constant time pressure.

That money will need to cover:

- Set up and compliance costs for your new company
- Paid marketing e.g. pay-per-click ads, your website, brochure or printing costs, etc.
- Marketing meetings. If you join a networking group or attend ad hoc meetings, there will be associated costs: transport, coffee and meals, and some groups also charge membership and attendance fees
- Training to address skill gaps—especially sales and marketing if you know you're weak in those areas
- Incidentals such as buying a laptop, a printer, setting up a home office, etc.

However much money you have at the start, one thing is true: unless you start to generate revenue, there's a lot more money in the first month than there is in later months. As a result, many new executives are tempted to spread their limited budget equally across months. That's a mistake, and its one that can kill your business very quickly. What you need to do instead is to invest more in the early months so that you build momentum and start bringing in cash as quickly as you can, but spend your money wisely.

If this is all new to you, then it's easy to spend money in the early stages on things that seem necessary but aren't. The best advice we can give you is to only spend money when it is *critical* for setting up, and focus on investments that support finding clients and creating stability and certainty.

How to finance yourself

We've established what costs you're going to need to cover, and the fact that you need to cover it for a year. So, how do you fund it?

It starts well in advance, while you're still in a permanent role. Plan ahead and set money aside. Decide ahead of time whether you're going to dip into existing savings, or you want to keep those back and build your war chest from scratch.

Money may come from a redundancy package from the role you're in. It may come from your partner's earnings if they have a job or an established business of their own. Some of our executives have a side business that is already profitable or an established business that they were running with their significant other.

One source that we don't recommend is debt—whether you take out a loan or rack up your credit cards.

Borrowing to fund your business creates more pressure, and any money left over after your living expenses gets swallowed up in debt repayments so it's harder to feel like you're getting ahead.

Be realistic

There's a tendency for new business owners—including new portfolio executives—to be overoptimistic and assume that they'll be the exception to the rule; that they'll be up and running much faster than the norm. Maybe you will, but you can't afford to assume that will be the case. It's better to under-promise and over-deliver—even to yourself. When you can see your funds running out and the clock is ticking, it forces you to make decisions on the fly, and you may not make the best choices. It's tempting to take on any client who is willing to pay you, even if the fee is too low or the work is outside your experience.

Adapting to life on your own

The portfolio lifestyle is very different from being an employee. All the structure and order that a job forces on you are gone, and you have to find your own path with your own rules and ways of working. There are no regular hours, and the boundaries between work and non-work can easily become blurred. Even when you haven't got

clients, you're always "on", thinking about work, or planning in your head. And when you do have clients, they
will want to call you outside normal office hours as well.
That can be hard for some people to adapt to—particularly if they have come up through a profession that likes
structure and order and clear guidelines and processes.

There are a couple of things you can do to make the transition easier.

First, find a buddy to keep you going. You need someone
on your side, reminding you that it's the calls and the contact that will get you the clients. Sara kept going because
she had Colin reaffirming that it works.

Second, set yourself activity targets—for example, calling
five new people every day—and be rigorous about following through.

Make your own structure

Since there's no outside party imposing structure on you,
you are free to structure your own time. Initially, your activities will be about putting in place the essentials you
need to operate, like setting up the business and equip-
ping your home office. Once that's done, your focus
should be on finding your first clients. Organize your time
around finding opportunities through your network—

your address book, family and friends, old colleagues, social activities.

Concentrate on having sixteen meetings per week—four a day from Monday to Thursday—with Fridays for catch-up and follow-up. And use every conversation as an opportunity to ask for a referral to two more people that could help you build your network.

That's more activity than most people anticipate, but initially it will take time to reignite old relationships and set up meetings. Once you're in the flow, however, and getting two additional referrals from each meeting, you'll have more than enough meetings to go to.

Many new entrepreneurs feel awkward talking to people they know about their new business because in their mind they're only doing it to get clients. To overcome that, when you're reigniting old relationships and meeting people, start the conversation by asking about them rather than talking about yourself. Most people like to talk about themselves, so the conversation will be easy and you'll find out a lot about that individual—what they're interested in, what their growth areas are, the pain points and opportunities they're facing—which will help you to position your new business and what you are trying to achieve.

Next, think about your purpose for being in business. If this is just about making money, and you're not passionate about building a new lifestyle and career or making a difference to your clients' lives, then people will probably pick up on the fact that you are only interested in getting clients. You'll come across as needy, which is not attractive. So, talk about why you've made the change, and what it means for the people you want to help. Then ask for help. Don't ask them to hire you, just to grow your network. The key is to be persistent and consistent in your daily activities. Be polite, do what you say you will, and follow up every introduction.

Technology

Most businesses today are dependent on technology, for everything from setting and managing appointments to communicating with prospects and clients. While setting that technology up can be daunting, the greater challenge by far is the security and compliance issues that arise, particularly when you're handling client data. It's important to stay on top of cybersecurity and data protection, and with smaller clients you may find yourself having to make them compliant too if they don't already have proper protocols and systems in place.

Of course, technology is always moving, and regulations change and evolve rapidly, so staying abreast of those developments and being able to introduce them at the right time to clients is challenging.

In your old full-time employee role, your organization probably had systems in place and a team of people to maintain those systems and support you. Once you go solo, those support structures are gone and you may become sharply aware of the gaps in your own technical knowledge and expertise. If you took a career break between leaving the corporate world and starting your own business, things may have changed dramatically in the meantime and it can feel intimidating to get back to it.

The basics

As a minimum, you'll need a decent laptop. Even if you have a desktop computer in your home office, you'll need a laptop that you can take with you to client meetings and work virtually with. You need to own and know how to use Microsoft Office, because that is what 99% of clients will be using. You will also need platforms to manage your diary, your marketing, and your social media.

Finally, communication software, especially video conferencing, is essential in a virtual world, and you may often be the one introducing that to your clients. Inside the Liberti companies, for example, we use a video meeting platform called Zoom for internal meetings and also for talking to clients when we are not in their offices.

All of that also means that you either need to know how to set those up yourself, or you need to find someone with technical expertise to help you get set up and to support you day-to-day.

That could be your teenage child or other relative, or you may have to agree a support package with a local IT provider. Support may also be available through professional associations and institutes, through organizations that support entrepreneurs setting up businesses, or through a local business incubator.

Being a self-starter

Most professionals think of themselves as self-starters. Very few think they need to be prodded and goaded into doing work. The proof—either way—is in what you get done each day and how much, rather than what you are thinking or saying.

Because portfolio executives don't have a boss setting objectives and telling them what to do—either day-to-day or over the year—it's essential to be a self-starter to succeed in this business. That means being curious, showing initiative, trying things out, being prepared to go outside of your comfort zones and do new things in new ways, and learning from your mistakes.

Being active and proactive—getting stuff done—is a key part of building your own business so you keep your diary full of meetings and events to go to. Even if you were a prolific self-starter in the corporate world, you might still find that once you're on your own, your productivity and initiative go down. You're moving into a new way of working, doing things you've never done before, many of which are firmly outside your comfort zone. So, it's natural that your fear begins to get in the way. That's when you can start to second-think yourself and succumb to paralysis by analysis. Over time, however, things will become familiar and move inside your new, expanded comfort zone, and you become productive again.

In reality, failure in this situation simply gives you more information about the right way to do things. The market will give you feedback on what you're doing and how. The key is not to keep doing the same things over and over again if they're not working.

Build a business plan

A critical element of your productivity is a plan that you can follow and that keeps you taking action. Set goals and objectives that you can use to track progress, and break them down into months, weeks, and days. Use short-term goals so that you can feel you're achieving something tangible, and longer-term goals to set direction. And give yourself rewards when you achieve your goals.

Once its ready, share your plan with others—family, friends, other business owners—and ask them to check in on how you're doing. That will create accountability. Your family, in particular, will be keenly interested in your plan!

1) Start with the culture, as we discussed earlier: What is your vision for the business? Your purpose? Your values?
2) Ask yourself where you want to be in a year's time.
3) Work back from there to set realistic milestones to reach that end goal.
4) Use those to set activity targets.

For example, you might decide that your one-year goal is: *I would like four clients who I am culturally aligned with, and to be working four days a week—one day a week with each one—with a day off for admin, top-up work, or to do something completely different.*

If you have to win four clients by the end of the year, at what stage will you bring each one on? Perhaps you will aim for one each quarter.

Then how many meetings do you need to have to get a client to say yes? Let's say you assume a 20% conversion rate—one "yes" for every five sales meetings you have. That means you need to have five sales meetings each quarter, so ask yourself what level of activity you need in order to generate those five meetings. What networking groups will you attend? How many referral relationships will you set up?

At this point, you need to do a sense-check. That could easily end up being a hundred meetings to generate five sales meetings to get one client. In the early weeks, when you're new to the market and no-one knows you, that would probably be hard. If you can get to a run rate of sixteen meetings a week after that initial period, however, then 100 meetings in the first quarter is achievable.

It will be hard at the start because the market will be testing you and it'll feel like you're doing lots of outbound calls and meetings with little reward. But, if you start giving to your network—connecting people with similar interests, helping people who have queries, thinking about individuals—reciprocity will kick in and people will start calling back with opportunities for you.

As you start to work your plan, check in with yourself every week. What have you done in the last seven days? What results did you get? What will you do over the next seven days? Focus on lead indicators like the number of initial outbound calls you're making or how many meetings you're setting up.

Over time, you'll get a good understanding of your ratios: how many calls you have to make to get a meeting, how many initial meetings you need to get a sales meeting, how many sales meetings to get a sale.

In addition, you should track follow-up activities. As your level of activity rises, so will the amount of follow-up you need to do. As that happens, it gets easier to "drop the ball" and start losing out on opportunities, so you'll need to systematize your follow-up activities. You should set up some sort of CRM system—even if it's just a spreadsheet.

Trust

It's hard for a new business with no track record to build trust. If you're new to town or building new relationships with people you don't know, they have nothing to fall back on; you're starting from scratch with them, building trust one day at a time.

> In the early days, a local bank manager said to Sara, "I'd love you to help our clients, but I don't know you."
>
> Because he was open about his doubts rather than simply saying, "I'll call you later," Sara was able to ask, "So, how can we make it happen?"
>
> They brainstormed some ideas, and in the end, Sara agreed to fill in at client events. He had a box at the local football club where he would entertain clients.

> Sometimes he couldn't fill the box, and Sara would go along at the last minute to make up the numbers.
>
> It ended up being one of the best decisions she made. It allowed her to get to know the bank manager better, but also she got to know everyone else in the box—his clients—and build relationships.
>
> Eventually, they started to ask her to do work for them.

Of course, trust has to work both ways: the executive has to also trust the client. Often, as a professional, you're worried that clients aren't telling you everything. Sometimes, you start working with a new client only to discover that the situation isn't what you were told. Suddenly, it's your reputation on the line—especially if you got the work through your network.

Getting paid

There are basically two ways to get paid for the work you are doing. You either get paid for work you are going to do in the future, or you get paid for work you have done in the past. If your client insists on being billed at the end of the month, you are trusting that they will be good for the money

Trusted partners

And finally, you need to trust your partner businesses. One of the most valuable resources you can offer your clients is access to a network of trusted partners and service providers that you can refer them to. When a client hires someone because you recommended them, your reputation and standing with them are on the line, so it's natural to feel a little anxiety around whether that partner will deliver a great service, even if they've done it in the past.

Chapter 9

Part of Something Bigger

Portfolio working can take many forms—as a "single shingle", as one of a small collective of individuals collaborating loosely, or as part of something bigger. In this chapter we describe the Liberti Group in more detail: a global organization creating the future of work through a team-based portfolio lifestyle for professionals.

We are seeing major changes in the world around how individuals want to engage in their work, and balance that with other parts of their lives. Increasingly, people are abandoning traditional employment models, and setting up their own businesses. One of the most popular ways of achieving that is the "gig economy", which individuals are using to gain more flexibility and control over their lives.

At the same time, however, being a freelancer in the gig economy isn't enough for many professionals because it doesn't meet our basic human needs to "belong"—to be part of a group—and to be part of something bigger than ourselves that can have real impact in the world. That is why the Liberti Group businesses are team-based.

The Liberti Story—Part 1: The FD Centre

We started the original Liberti business, The FD Centre, because we were looking for a different way of working ourselves, one where we weren't "owned" by a corporation and forced to follow their agenda. We saw an opportunity to do things differently and run our own agenda, building our own portfolio of clients. And we saw a gap in the SME market, where businesses needed our skills but they didn't need us all the time. We just had to find a way to deliver those skills in smaller units and service a portfolio of clients.

We also realized that there must be others like us, and more SMEs that needed someone but had no idea where to find them other than hiring a full-time director. Bringing those two sides together was the start of the business. It gave us variety in our work and—because we weren't working with one client all the time—we were able to experience new challenges and different sectors. And the team environment we created satisfied our needs for belonging and being part of something bigger than ourselves.

Initially, Colin wasn't sure whether the focus would be just on finance or would extend to broader management skills. He could see SMEs had a need for the wider skill set, but he had learnt the hard way that it was easier to get clients as a specialist than as a generalist.

From 2001 to 2005, when Sara joined, the business consisted of Colin testing the model, building his own portfolio, and proving the concept. He had a vision of turning it into a full-fledged business, but he wanted to make sure it would work at an individual level first before asking anyone else to make the jump. As we saw earlier, the strength of Sara's position was that she wasn't totally dependent on fee earning, so she was able to devote time to growing the business and bring in more clients than she and Colin could serve. So, bringing her into the company made it possible to scale the team rapidly into a real business, and fulfil Colin's vision.

By the end of 2005 there were four of us leading the business, each with our own portfolio but working as a team and sharing what we were learning about how to find, win, and keep clients. More importantly, however, we realized early on that there were two types of professionals: those who wanted to focus on client work, and those who wanted to build the business. So, we started to bring in other executives who wanted to work purely on delivery while the rest of us were happy to bring in clients for them.

The Liberti Story—Part 2: Expanding the Footprint

As The FD Centre grew, we realized that the single centralized team structure that had helped us grow was stopping us from expanding any further. That is when we created the Regional Director role that is still at the heart of our business development activities, and Colin, Sara and the others each took responsibility for growing local teams in an allocated region.

By 2009, we wanted to take the model overseas. The business was still relatively small, with just £5m turnover, and we had only just achieved national coverage in the UK, so international expansion was a major leap—and potentially a leap too far.

We were working with an Australian business coaching firm who encouraged us to think that the model would work in Australia and helped us to find someone to be our country leader there. The financial cost of starting up was low—the business model depends primarily on intellectual capital in the form of business processes and the knowledge we have built up—so our biggest investment was time.

After Australia, we copied the same model to launch South Africa, then Canada, Singapore, Belgium and the Netherlands, and Sara took responsibility for mentoring all the country leaders on how to build the business in their countries. Being first to market in those countries means we were the ones who got to educate the market about portfolio executives, which was a major competitive advantage.

What was fascinating was the realization that in every country you find the same senior professionals looking to swap the restrictions of the corporate world for freedom, flexibility, variety, and control, but still want to belong and be part of a team. And in every country, you also find SMEs and entrepreneurs with the same issues, who have grown too big to survive without executive-level skills but aren't yet big enough to afford them full-time.

Today, The FD Centre (known in some countries as The CFO Centre) has 600 portfolio finance executives in sixteen countries, and the Liberti group has expanded into other fields, as we'll explain.

The Liberti Story—Part 3: More than Finance

In 2011, we started to wonder whether we could apply the same model not just to new countries, but to new disciplines like IT or marketing.

As soon as we started to talk about it in the market, we attracted Lucy and Clare, who started The Marketing

Centre. They had just left an agency and wanted to build something, but they didn't want it to be another traditional agency. They had seen what we were doing in finance and thought *Wouldn't it be good to do that but in marketing.*

After The Marketing Centre, we added an IT business (Freeman Clarke), HR (People Puzzles), bookkeeping and financial control (Your Right Hand), legal advice (My Inhouse Lawyer), and sales (Kiss The Fish). In total, we have over 1,000 executives across 7 disciplines in 16 countries.

Who this is not for

Becoming a portfolio executive in a Liberti company is not for everyone.

First, of course, you have to ask yourself whether the lifestyle of a portfolio executive is right for you.

You also have to want to be part of a team because that is the core of our business model.

Most importantly from our point of view, you have to be someone who will fit in with our culture and is aligned with our values: open, progressive and passionate.

And finally, you have to be someone who is looking to build a portfolio business, not just an interim role while you wait for a permanent offer.

Are You Ready for the Next Step?

The portfolio executive lifestyle is not for everyone. If you're reading this book, however, and this sounds interesting, then we would love to talk to you.

To start the conversation, visit
www.TheLibertiGroup.com/getstarted

Making the Transition

The role of the Liberti Group is to make the transition from employee to portfolio executive as smooth as possible. Once we've selected an individual for a Liberti Group company, we take them through an intake process and teach them our IP.

Whichever Liberti brand someone is joining, the process starts with induction, then a transition into field work and working in their regional team.

The intake process lasts up to a year, so if you're unwilling or unable to give it a year and keep yourself going, this is probably not the right choice for you. On the other hand, if you are able to work through those initial months, we have taken hundreds of executives through the intake process all over the world, so we know it works.

Of course, the end of the intake process is not the end of your professional development. You'll know how to operate the business model, but you still have to stay at the top of your game in your discipline. So, each Liberti company provides extensive development opportunities for its executives.

Our partners are very keen to work with us and support us. Through them, we are able to offer technical training at the company and team level, so you can brush up on technical skills, learn about new products in the market, new regulation, compliance etc.

At a team level, we also offer ongoing training on the commercial aspects of the business. What joining a Liberti Group company does is to future-proof your career by giving you the skills you need to get to market. Once you have them, they are with you for life and you continue to learn how to find, win, and keep clients within your team, with your colleagues and mentors, and an allocated buddy.

Throughout the process, you also have access to the professional knowledge and experience of everyone in the group, along with the various platforms which hold all our IP around the business model.

None of this, of course, works if you don't take responsibility for your own development. We respond to the needs of our executives, but it's up to you to take advantage of the opportunities we create for you.

Support for Finding

Alongside personal and professional development opportunities, one of the big advantages of joining a Liberti Group company is the support the group gives executives for finding, winning, and keeping clients.

Now, don't misunderstand. Liberti Group is not your personal pipe-line. It is a business which teaches you how to build your portfolio within our team environment.

This is about learning to fish, not having fish fed to you. However, marketing channels change and evolve over time. New opportunities and trends arise all the time, and it is our responsibility within all the businesses in the Liberti Group to keep looking ahead, developing channels and identifying the opportunities, testing them and systematizing them so they work, and then bringing them to bear directly within each of the businesses.

We do a lot of marketing that very few executives would do for themselves. First, it's too time-consuming. Second, it's too expensive. And third, unless they're in marketing, it's not something they're likely to be passionate about or competent at.

In our business model, 10% of revenue is set aside to run the business. Depending on the company, between a quarter and a half of that is spent on marketing—that's millions of dollars of marketing investment every year on behalf of our executives.

Anyone can post a few Tweets or write a handful of articles. It's harder to scale that and turn it into a machine that keeps running and delivers, which is what we do for our executives.

Support for winning

Within the Liberti Group, the regional director role is focussed on winning new clients. While they also spend time engaging the team and meeting potential executives, a quarter of their time is dedicated to winning clients for the team.

In practice, individual executives find many of the opportunities themselves. However, whether an opportunity has come from an executive or through the corporate activities, it is the regional director who owns and drives the winning process. That means that once you've identified a potential client, you have hands-on support from an expert in sales—an area which is outside the strengths of most professionals.

Through the recruitment and onboarding process, regional directors get to know the executives in their team thoroughly: what clients might suit them, and what kind of clients they are looking for in their portfolio. That understanding deepens over time as the regional director and the executive work together on finding activities—the more time they can spend together, the better—and building a personal business plan for the executive.

In addition to support from their regional director, if a principal is struggling to engage and win clients we'll pay for a sales coach to work with them and get them through their blocks. Both sides have invested a lot of time, money, and effort to get this far, and we want them to succeed.

Support for Keeping

Ultimately, the key to keeping a client is to give them what they want and keep delivering value. Over the years, we've learned what clients are looking for from their executives, and how the relationship and their needs evolve over time.

All our executives are trained on the client lifecycle, how to create work plans to engage with the client, and how to get into a rhythm with them so you are meeting their needs over the long term. There are specific things clients need at each stage in the lifecycle, and we train our executives to deliver that to the client and get them to where they need to go.

We also support them by gathering feedback from all our clients. After the third and twelfth months, and annually after that, every client has a call with a client experience manager who is outside the local team structure. If appropriate, the results are shared with the executive and their regional director, so they can have an open conversation around progress. This isn't a performance review. Often, the feedback from the client is overwhelmingly positive and focused on what's working well. And if there is something that the client isn't happy with, it's an opportunity for them to bring it up so the executive can do something about it.

Ultimately, if you're good at what you do, then you have nothing to fear from feedback. So, we look for people who welcome feedback and see it as an opportunity to learn vs anything else.

Team Support

The team environment we have created gives our executives access to support and collaboration that they would not have as independents. It also provides the ability to expand their offer to clients both in terms of skill set and geographically.

That's a powerful differentiator in the market. Across the different Liberti brands, we have a number of clients that operate in multiple locations and were attracted to our ability to deliver a single skill set to them everywhere that they operate. It's an attractive value proposition because they are working with a set of people who already work as a team and have solved the challenges of collaboration, coordination, and standardization. Equally, we have clients who have hired us in a single location to deliver multiple professional disciplines such as finance, IT, marketing, etc.

As well as encouraging executives to look for opportunities to introduce other skill sets or geographies, we hold conferences and client events that bring together all the Liberti brands. That allows us to grow the scope of existing clients and find new ways to deliver value to them.

Building relationships internally

One of the challenges we face is that our executives are physically isolated from their colleagues, with no central office for people to gather in and meet each other the way they would in a corporate role or a professional services firm. To counter that, we have a very deliberate process for helping our executives to build relationships with each other.

All the Liberti business, as we've discussed earlier in the book, operate in regional teams of up to twenty principals, so there's a sense of 'home' and 'belonging' to a team. Within that team, there's a rhythm of activities to bring everyone together regularly. The meetings aren't all business, however. They normally include something social as well. So a typical team meeting will include an element of training, a regional progress update, working on client activities, and something for people to get to know each other better. In addition, every business also has two national conferences each year that bring all its teams together.

As well, each executive stays in regular contact with the cohort of people who joined at the same time and have been going through onboarding at the same time. They go through training and induction together, then return to their regional teams.

Finally, we encourage executives to build their own personal connections. We have an online mapping tool that allows executives to identify all the other executives in a local region across all the Liberti companies, so they can support each other on the ground.

As a virtual business, technology plays a major role in how we communicate and engage with each other. Increasingly, we've found that once the face-to-face, physical relationship has been built, it's easier to move it online. It's more efficient, and it means executives don't have to travel long distances to meet.

Leadership

In most corporations, it's hierarchy that holds everything together and drives everything from strategy to communication. In Liberti, we don't rely on command and control. In its place, our shared culture is the glue that holds the business together.

We consider all our people to be leaders in their field, so Liberti companies have a relatively flat structure with little or no hierarchy. However, leadership happens at every level.

We have a global leadership team that shares the vision, the purpose and the values. Below that we have country leaders, and regional directors below them who lead our teams.

The most important leadership relationship we have, however, is with our clients. As portfolio executives, our role is to lead our clients towards their objectives. We lead the function we have been hired into, but also we are often the most experienced leader in the organization, and clients look to us for more than functional leadership.

Individuals join us because they are aligned with our vision of the future of work and our purpose of making a difference. They can see they fit in with our culture and they are inspired by, and want to follow, the leadership path we have set.

While our flat structure is what distinguishes us from a professional services firm, it's the leadership we do have in place that sets us apart from an agency. We are not just a database of 1,000 people looking for clients and sharing support and resources for expediency. We have direction and vision, and a shared culture, and that is what gives the work we do meaning.

The Liberti Culture

Our vision in the Liberti group is to create a whole new way of working—the team-based portfolio lifestyle—and redefine the future of work for professionals. Our purpose is to make a real difference to our lives, the lives of our members, and the lives of our clients by working that way.

Our culture is built around three core values: "open", "progressive", and "passionate". These guide how we behave in our business and in our lives.

Open is about caring and being real. When you're working with entrepreneurs, everything you do affects real money and real lives. So, you have to "tell it like it is", share the whole truth, and be straightforward in your dealings with people—the clients, the partners, and the staff. At the same time, it has to be done in a caring way, with the best intent for the individual.

Progressive is critical for us because we are creating a new industry in a new market with a new business model. We are constantly learning and growing about how to evolve this business model, and we want the professionals who join us to be people who are prepared to learn and grow, who are not afraid to step out of their comfort zone to try new things and learn new skills to change their career.

Passionate is about bringing energy, excitement, and enthusiasm to every situation rather than sucking it out. We want other people to look forward to us coming in when we show up to meetings with our team or our clients.

Fairness and trust

The Liberti model is a high-trust model—that's what has allowed us to grow without the command and control structures an organization of this size and scope usually demands. We didn't want to build a business around dealing with the lowest common denominator. Instead, we assumed we would attract like-minded people who fit our culture and really wanted to work this way, and we would trust that they could do the job, were properly trained, and would invest extra time to get trained up and keep their skills current as necessary.

That allowed us to create a low-process organization very different from the corporate environments our executives are escaping from. People don't want to fill in forms and have someone checking on them all the time, so we work on the basis of self-responsibility. When things go wrong—which, of course, they occasionally do—we don't jump back into a command control and process to fix it. Instead, we treat it as a sign that the person probably isn't the right fit.

Rather than building the process around people, we choose people around the process we have. When you have the right people, whom you trust, in the right teams, you don't need to tie the organization up with a lot of process activity, checking, and controlling.

We also apply high trust to our relationships with partners and clients. We are a relationship business, and we try to minimize the amount of documentation. For example, rather than signing a detailed contract, a partnership with a new distribution partner might be captured in a single sheet that sets out what we are looking to achieve together. The focus is on getting started to see how everyone behaves and whether there's a fit.

Our client contracts are similarly brief—a single sheet with terms and conditions—and we don't ask our executives to submit timesheets. The agreement is a commitment from the client that they are going to engage with us and that they will pay a certain amount for that service. Each month, the executive liaises with the client in advance to agree what work needs to be done, and we invoice the client for the work that will be done.

Income sharing

Liberti businesses are not franchises. There's no joining fee, and the executives who join us don't pay fees to stay in the business.

Client invoicing is done centrally in each Liberti business, and when a client pays their invoice, the revenue is split between the executive who did the work, their regional director, and the Liberti business. The exact split depends on which business the executive is in, but everyone in that company will get the same percentage. There are no side deals: when you sit with a colleague in a team meeting or a company conference, you know they haven't negotiated a better deal for themselves than you got.

The regional director's share is designed to reward them for their coordination role and the support they provide in finding and winning clients for the team.

The company's share reflects the central marketing activities they undertake, the training and development they provide, and the administrative support they give to executives.

Our aim was to create a business model where executives who join us are no worse off than if they stayed independent, and in reality the level of support they get means that they are much better off. Especially since Liberti group executives are typically able to achieve higher day rates than if they went to market on their own.

Authenticity and Values

If you've got this far in the book, you understand how important authenticity and strong values are to us.

We left the corporate world because we wanted to get away from the politics and games, and inauthentic leadership. We wanted to be able to be ourselves, show up fully in our business, and connect with entrepreneurs who also want to show up fully in their business. We recognized that we needed to have strong values to show what we stood for, and we worked hard to define those early on: Open, Progressive, and Passionate.

With 1,000 people in the Liberti Group, it's hard work to stop politics from creeping in, but our executives are more likely to encounter it in their clients than inside the company. To keep it at bay internally, we've adopted an approach of openness and sharing our whole truth around issues, which is a tool that encourages having real conversations rather than holding onto resentment and not unblocking energy blocks.

Are You Ready for the Next Step?

The portfolio executive lifestyle is not for everyone. If you've read this book, however, and this is what you want, then I encourage you to go for it.

If you also think you'd be a fit culturally for one of the Liberti Group companies, and you want the support of a team then we would love to talk to you.

To start the conversation, visit
www.TheLibertiGroup.com/getstarted

Index

44121940R00154

Made in the USA
Middletown, DE
03 May 2019